My Brother's Keeper

Church Ministry for Young
African American Males

Dr. Samuel White, III,

WESTBOW®
PRESS
A DIVISION OF THOMAS NELSON
& ZONDERVAN

WestBow Press books may be ordered through booksellers or by contacting:

WestBow Press
A Division of Thomas Nelson & Zondervan
1663 Liberty Drive
Bloomington, IN 47403
www.westbowpress.com
1 (866) 928-1240

ISBN: 978-1-4908-4938-6 (sc)
ISBN: 978-1-4908-4939-3 (hc)
ISBN: 978-1-4908-4940-9 (e)

Library of Congress Control Number: 2014916544

Printed in the United States of America.

WestBow Press rev. date: 10/28/2014

Contents

Acknowledgements.. ix

Foreword.. xiii

Introduction..xvii

Chapter 1   Social Chains of Young African American Males.............. 1

Chapter 2   Psychological Chains of Young African American Males.... 20

Chapter 3   Spiritual Chains of Young African American Males........ 38

Chapter 4   Liberation of The Laity 59

Chapter 5   Liberation Ministries 90

Chapter 6   Transforming Trouble Makers Into Peacemakers.......... 137

Chapter 7   Liberating Lyrics...169

Chapter 8   Liberating Parents...212

Bibliography... 249

About the Author 253

TO JESUS CHRIST,

OUR LORD, SAVIOR

AND LIBERATOR WH0

SETS THE CAPTIVES FREE

Acknowledgements

I am indebted to our Lord and Savior Jesus Christ who liberated my soul from sin, death and damnation. It is only through Him that I was able to write this book and He deserves all the praise. In spite of my procrastination, accidently erasing three chapters, He patiently worked with me and enabled me to complete this work. I praise God for my 2:00 am writing sessions with our Lord.

I must acknowledge the members of my former congregation, Trinity Faith United Methodist Church who helped me to conduct this ministry. Thanks to the Pastor Parish Relations Committee, Terrance King, Steve McElroy, Roderick McCain, Rev. Magnum, Ed Oliver, Danny Peeples, Antoinette Gillespie, Bernard Spragnor, Rick Thomas, Eric Lee, Rev. Wallace and Mr. and Mrs. Verdun M.D.s for being workers, counselors, coaches, and group discussion leaders. I am especially grateful for the "street wisdom" of ex-drug dealers, gang members and street people. They gave me an education that no professor, scholar, book or university could ever give.

I praise God for my present congregation, Friendship Baptist who allowed me the support and time to fulfill this project. I especially want to acknowledge the Sunday School, Youth Group, After School program, College Boosters, My Brothers' Keeper Mentoring program, Christian Basketball League, Scholarship Committee, and the Mission ministry for their work among youth, adolescence and the needy. God bless your ministries.

I am thankful for academic support of Dr. Herbert Douglass, Dr. Marcella Mc Donald, Dr. Carlyle Stewart, Dr. Arthur Pressly, Dr. Dey, Dr. Aymer and other faculty members at Drew University Theological School who have been a source of support in many germinal ideas. I am also thankful for Dr. Charles Adams, Dr. Harvey Cox and the late Dr. Peter Gomes of Harvard University who inspired me to strive beyond the realm of mediocrity into educational excellence.

I am extremely grateful for my faithful friends that have been so supportive. I have truly been blessed with outstanding colleagues in ministry like, Rev. Foster, Rev. Issa, Rev. Greer-Stevens, Rev. Clark, Minister Bean, Rev. Stevens, Dr. Beverly, Dr. Bulloch, Dr. Perkins and Dr. Stewart. God has blessed me with friendships that I didn't deserve. I am eternally grateful for the written endorsements of Dr. Perkins, Dr. Nabors and Dr.Turman. Thank you my friends. A special thanks for the service and conflict resolution information of our Jamaican missionary Rev. Peek Vary.

Lastly, I could not have completed this book without the undying love and faith of my family. Thanks for the unflappable spirit of my mother Anna White who taught me to smile in the face of adversity, the tenacious spirit of my late father Samuel, who inspired me to climb mountains, and the wisdom of my older brother David who mentored me into manhood. I cannot thank God enough for my big brothers love and guidance. Also, I praise God for the creativity of my older sister Dee Ann, the charismatic, dynamic leadership of my sister Cherise', the bold, beautiful spirit of my younger sister Renee' and the passion for justice of my younger brother Van. It is their characteristics that have helped to make me the person I am today. Mere words cannot express my enormous gratitude. Thanks to my late mother- in- law Mildred and brother- in- law Donnie who jump started me into writing again. I thank God for my wonderful wife Sandra who had more faith in me than I *had in myself.* In spite of my doubts and insecurities, she sees greatness in me. She is the "wind beneath my wings." In the immortal words of Stevie Wonder, "I will be loving you always…" Thanks to my precocious daughter Alexandria, who patiently taught this technically challenged preacher how to work on this lap top computer. She endured my bouts of frustration and without her I could not have finished this work. She is destined for greatness. I am grateful to my sensational son Samuel IV who inspired and informed me about some of the contents of this book. His insights about the influences of Rap music and video games was extremely valuable. His critique of some of the Liberation Lessons, Liberating Lyrics and the Peacemaker program was very helpful. I am proud of the teenager he is and the man that he is becoming. My family is more than the love of my life. They are my life. Finally ,thanks to the countless, unnamed people who have challenged , comforted , mentored , taught , disciplined , sacrificed , worked , patiently waited and prayed for me all throughout my life. If I did not mentioned your name, charge it to my head and not my heart. I am truly thankful for whatever you have done for me. For I know it was God that was working through you to develop my soul and give me this wonderful life. Praise the Lord.

Foreword

"My Brothers' Keeper, Church Ministry to Young African American Males ", premise is exceptional and the work follows it all the way through. That is, "What has happened to our young African American males?" The cadre of questions Dr. White goes on to pose in the introduction are almost catastrophic. Especially telling are the following; what are the social factors that influence the baneful behavior of young African American males? How does the drug culture influence our young people? In what way has the public school failed them? To what extent does teen unemployment lead to criminal behavior? What are the psychological factors that affect Black males? This is the meat of the book, in that its presentation is a sort of a diametric juxtaposition surrounding each of these questions. The book not only answers Cains' question, "Am I my brothers' keeper?" but develops 1) a brilliant overall structure encompassing the challenges facing young black males, 2) a history and instruction regarding the elements of the structure from an African American religious point of view 3) a theological response to the structure designed to destroy black males and to counter it with a church-based solution.

The structural framework of the book is strong and easy to follow; social chains, psychological chains, and spiritual chains are all endemic woes keeping young black males in bondage and or leading them into bondage. The information is precise and supported by critical evaluation of demographic, statistical and probing analysis of the available resources.

Chapter one sets the table in evaluating the historical and current socioeconomic issues that have kept young black males in bondage. Dr. Whites' empirical conclusions about the role of the church are compelling and disturbing. Chapter two seeks to enter the fray of mental distress and challenge as it relates to social, family, and spiritual realities facing young black males. Chapter three describes the different aspects of spiritual chains; church, family Media, Rap music. The information on the church and spiritual sickness is as painful and abhorrent as it is precise and specific. Dr. White writes, "The church is sick in our complacency and judgement." At this point it almost appears the picture he has painted is overwhelming, with no hope that things will improve.

However, the remainder of the book, Chapter four "Liberating the Laity" , Chapter five, "Liberating Ministries" , Chapter six, "Transforming Troublemakers into Peacemakers" , Chapter seven, "Liberating Lyrics" and Chapter eight "Liberating Parents" present an option, a way an opportunity to address the quagmire of structural issues that have diseased our young black males.

Dr. White places the Black Church squarely front and center, regarding the endangered species known as the "black male." Unapologetically claiming that the Black Church possess as much of the blame on the current state of Black males as any other sector of society, White then offers building blocks of hope that can break the socio/economic, psychological, and spiritual chains from the liberation of our young black males.

He utilizes a life of ministry on the front lines and critical thinking of Harvard Divinity School training, to address one of the most critical issues of the day. Dr. Whites' passion rings through on nearly every page as he uncovers the actions, behavior and thinking of young black males caught in a vicious cycle of poverty, drug culture, violence and hopelessness. He then counters each reality with a solid, biblical remedy that is available for every local church committed to reaching young black males.

This is a must read for any church; white, black, suburban, urban or rural, who is dedicated in ushering constructive, Godly change into the African

American community. I pray every pastor in America reads and uses Whites' work. Maybe then the nascent trends of subjugation can truly lead to liberation for us all.

Dr. Michael Nabors, Senior Pastor, New Calvary Baptist Church,
Detroit Michigan
Director of the M.Div. Program at the Ecumenical Theological
Seminary, Detroit Michigan

Introduction

I will never forget the day when I caught a young African American male urinating against the back wall of the church. I was completely disgusted and disturbed by this gross spectacle of disrespect against the House of God. I sternly spoke to the young man, "Hey young man, you can use the bathroom inside of the church." He responded, "I didn't know it was a church... it don't matter." I quickly retorted, "What did you mean it doesn't matter?" He started to walk away. I yelled out to him, "Hey pull up your pants!" The young man glared at me, mumbled something under his breath and walked away with his pants still sagging.

What has happened to our young African American males? Why are some of them so disrespectful to others and to themselves? Why do they let their pants sag showing their underwear and low self-esteem? How is it that an innocent little boy could grow up to be a lying, stealing, drug dealing, gun-toting, thug terrorizing our neighborhood? How it is that todays' Cain is killing his brother Able?

Nationally, African American males are 3 % of the population but are an astounding 50% of all violent crimes! The principal killer among Detroit's young African American males is guns and drugs. In Detroit, it was reported that, nine out of ten murders of African American children were gun and drug related. In Detroit, one of every five-hundred African American males from ages fifteen to eighteen were murdered. [1] Young people in this age group are almost twice as likely to die of homicide as of all other causes combined. Youth homicide surely is a public emergency. Many African American juveniles have been maimed or murdered because of drug dealing. Dr. Melvin Gyer, an associate professor in psychiatry and psychology for twenty-two years at the University of Michigan, says:" It is a new phenomenon as we watch the age of juvenile criminals increasingly go down, down, down and severity of their crimes go up. The kids we are seeing now do not form any type of psychiatric disorder. They are simply products of their environment and are functioning quite well in their own little worlds. They are very much like children who grow up in a war zones. Survival—looking out for number one is the only thing that matters." [2]

Unfortunately many young African American males are not surviving. They are what Dr. Gibbs refers to as the "Endangered Species." Young Black males are incarcerated, drug addicted, emasculated and exterminated at an early age. A sixty pound third-grader so small that Wayne County juvenile Court workers dub him the" Smurf" was charged with attempted murder in the stabbing of a nine year old over crack. A ten year-old believed to be the youngest drug dealer ever arrested in the Detroit area was found sitting on eleven packs of heroin and twenty-five rocks of crack during a police raid at his Detroit home. A sixteen year old broke into a home and threatened to kill a young woman's baby if she didn't give him some money for drugs. After the money was given and the car stolen, he was caught. Police arrested the youth finding nine rocks of crack cocaine in his underwear, a gold bracelet, four gold necklaces and three gold rings. Moreover the drug trade has brought about a lot of gang violence, bloodshed and killed countless numbers of innocent children and youth. A young woman in my church was abducted, thrown in a car trunk, killed and buried in a shallow grave by three young African American males. A young African American male member of my church was shot in the head by his cousin in a drug deal gone bad. These are just a few of the examples of the mayhem created by young African American males.

In Detroit, if African American youth are not killed they end up in jail or in prison. The Michigan Department of Corrections has estimated that there are between five to six thousand teenage offenders that come through the courts yearly. Moreover one out of four African American males end up in the criminal justice system. Most of them have either gone to prison or are on probation because of drug related activity.

The drug epidemic that is making Detroit a city of chaos and carnage has begun to effect the church and leave some parishioners drug addicted, depressed, and co-dependent. My former church was not immune from this socio-spiritual sickness. It was located in northwest Detroit. The community that surrounded the church had been plagued by criminal activity and violence stemming from the proliferation of drugs. The drug culture encompassing the church had an extremely detrimental effect on the psychological, spiritual and social well- being of young African American males. Their exposure to drugs had led to their crack cocaine addiction, incarceration, fragmentation of their family, criminalization , gang activity, identity crisis and spiritual slavery. One of the mothers of the church, whose son was addicted to heroin lamented, "What has happened to my boy and what can the church do to help? "

Unfortunately, there has been very little written specifically about adolescent African American male drug dealers, gangster and social deviants. They are a new sociological phenomena that is yet to be fully explored. There is even less literature written on how the church is to do ministry with young African American males. There is some related literature that deals with the particular problems of young black men. Reginald L. Jones work," The Black Adolescents", gives us an overview of contemporary Black adolescent from social, psychological, economic, educational, medical and historical perspectives. Jewell Taylor Gibbs book," Young, Black and Male in America", is helpful in presenting the complex constellation of mutually enforcing conditions that young black men confront. "The Dangerous Society", by Carl S. Taylor enlightens us on the youth gangs in the city of Detroit. Jwanza Kunjifu has written several books addressing the conspiracy to destroy Black boys and the need to motivate them with positive self- images. Van Henri White Esq. has written an outstanding book that reveals the anger and frustration young men feel as they confront Americas' structural injustices and inequalities. Dr. Perkins has written two very informative and inspirational books entitled," Rebuilding Zion's Walls" and "12 Plays for Boys". All of these books are very helpful and should be on every ones bookshelf.

Still, there is an enormous need for more research and study in this critical area. There are still too many unanswered questions. What are the social factors that influence the baneful behavior of young African American males? How does the drug culture influence our young people? In what way has the public schools failed them? To what extent does teen unemployment lead to criminal behavior? What are the psychological factors that affect Black males? Why do they have such a low self-esteem? How do peer groups and gangs influence the behavior of Black males? How does a paternal absenteeism or dysfunctional families affect their psyche? What are the spiritual factors that contribute to the demise of the young African American males? Where do young African American drug dealers get their values and ethics? How has Rap music and videos influenced their morality and spirituality? How is the church an unwitting accomplice to gang violence, drug dealing and the criminality of our youth? What can the church do to address the drug culture and gang violence that is destroying our young men? What ministries can the church offer to liberate young African American males? Should the church be involved in liberating addicts, thugs, gangsters, drug dealers, hustlers and carjackers? Or in the immortal words of Cain, "Am I my brothers' keeper?"

This book is dedicated to answering Cain's question and understanding the social, psychological and spiritual factors that develop young African American male drug dealers, substance abusers, gang members and social deviants. We must explore the depths of their depravity and captivity. The bible states, "You shall know the truth and the truth will set you free." I hope that some truth will be shed on young African American males, the families that raised them, the schools that failed to teach them, the gangs that socialized them, the drug culture that indoctrinated them, the society that discriminated against them, the corrupt media that brainwashed them and the church that unwittingly enslaved them. Once the "truth" is comprehended, the church can develop liberation ministries that ultimately set them free spiritually, psychologically and socially. The truth will not only liberate our youth, but also their parents and the laity.

Chapter one delineates the socioeconomic chains that contribute to the adolescent African American male's drug activity. What is the sociological portrait of the churches neighborhood and does it lead to criminal behavior? How does the public school system, unemployment, gangs and peer groups aid and abet this problem? What is the socialization process of the drug dealer? These and other questions will be asked as we understand the world of African American youth. Through surveys, interviews and research we can discover how society contributes to their demise.

Chapter two will examine the psychological chains that lead African American males to drug dealing and substance abuse. What influences give him an addictive mentality? Why do young Black males think and behave the way they do? Why are some of them so full of anger and violence? Why do they have such a low self-esteem? We will attempt to answer these and other questions through research, surveys and interviews. Their psychological development, self-perceptions, and their family will be addressed in this chapter.

Chapter three will assess the spiritual chains that may foster substance abuse among adolescent African American males. What shapes the moral development of adolescent African American males? What kind of faith does the drug dealer have? How has Rap music and television influenced their behavior? What kind of ethical code do they live by? What is their perception of the traditional church, preacher and God? How has the mainline church inadvertently contributed to the drug culture and fostered the spiritual chains of our youth? My research and interviews were helpful in answering these questions. This information enables us to understand the spiritual bondage of young black males.

Chapter four is entitled the Liberation of the Laity. Before the youth can be set free, the parents, youth workers and Sunday school teachers, must be set free from their prejudice, ageism, ignorance of youth culture, self-righteousness and antiquated youth ministries. The laity need to understand that," they are their brothers' keeper". They need to be trained in youth culture and the issues they confront. Moreover, the laity need to be enlightened about the healing liberation ministry of the church. There will be training sessions that will deal with the following topics: liberation of the mind, heart and soul; the psychological, social, spiritual perspective of young black males', substance abuse and biblical- theological foundation for youth ministry. These training sessions will equip the laity to become their brothers' keeper.

Chapter five provides liberation ministries for young African American males. This chapter will provide a step by step process in how to develop a mentoring program called, "My Brothers' Keeper". Also there is a Rites of Passage program and Liberation Lessons that address youth culture and raise their social, moral and psychological consciousness. These liberation ministries are designed to save souls, raise self –esteem, develop social consciousness, fulfill paternal depravation, and prepare our young men for this life and beyond.

Chapter six is entitled transforming troublemakers into peacemakers. Our youth will be introduced to the Prince of Peace Jesus Christ and the plan of salvation. Once they have accepted Jesus Christ as their Lord and Savior they will go through Christian Conflict Resolution Classes. These classes will help them deal with their anger, violence and conflicts. They will learn to be peacemakers in their home, school and amongst their peers. I believe that God can raise up a generation of peace makers to His glory.

Chapter seven is called Liberating Lyrics. One of the major ways to reach young African American males is through Rap Music. It is such an influential medium upon young African American males, that to ignore it or reject it in their liberation process would be a grave mistake. I believe that some rap music can be used to liberate the minds of our youth. Even the rap songs filled with profanity and vulgarities provide object lessons on what not to believe or practice. Liberating Lyrics are songs that can raise the spiritual and social conscious level of our kids and set them free from worldly lies and half-truths. Therefore I have researched the lyrics of rap, R@B, Hip Hop and Reggae music, wrote meditations and reflective questions based on those lyrics. The Sunday school teacher, youth worker or mentor can use these Liberating Lyrics in a group discussion format. They will discover that the youth will take a great interest when they're discussing some of their favorite songs and they will learn in the process. If we want to reach our youth, we must enter their world. We must meet our youth where they are, to lead them where they need to be. We can't liberate their minds, if we do not understand how they think. Liberating lyrics will give us insight about the perspective of our youth and spiritually enlighten them.

Chapter eight is entitled liberating the Parents. A young man enslaved by the drug culture, may mean the enslavement of his parents. Parents of drug addicted or troubled teenagers can be shackled to their poor parenting perspectives and their child's erratic baneful behavior. Consequently, parenting becomes an emotional, spiritual rollercoaster ride that can erode the spiritual vitality of the parent. In order for a parent to cope with their sons issues and experience peace of mind they must be liberated of their codependency and dysfunctional behaviors. The bible and spiritual wisdom is the key to their liberation process. This chapter sheds light on ten parenting dysfunctions and spiritual actions needed to rectify them. Also parents in the bible are profiled with their successes and failures. Finally there is a list of scriptures for parents that will give them spiritual strength and guidance.

If you are tired of watching our young men wearing sagging pants , rapping with profanity , using the "n" word , smoking marijuana , selling drugs ,having children out of wedlock , terrorizing our neighborhood , going to jail , killing one another, than it is time to get involved and be "My Brothers' Keeper." We need to stop crying and complaining and do something about it. For too long we have wallowed in apathy and fear while drugs, crime and violence runs rampant in our neighborhoods. For too long we have rejected, ignored or demonized young African American males and asked, "Am I my brothers' keeper?" It is time that we acknowledge the fact that, we are our brothers' keeper. Contrary to popular opinion these boys are not second-class citizens, monsters, strangers, demons or aliens. They are our sons, nephews, cousins, brothers and neighbors. It does not matter what they have done or who they are, we have a moral mandate to help them. It's time for Christians and people of goodwill to deny themselves, take up the cross, put on the whole Armor of God and fight the good fight. We need to respond to President Obamas' initiative and be "My Brothers' Keeper." It's time for us to obey the words of the prophet Amos, "Do justice love mercy and walk humbly with thy God." It's time for us take on the ministry of our Lord, "preach the gospel to the poor, heal the broken hearted, preach deliverance to the captives, recovering of sight to the blind and set at liberty them that are bruised."

"My Brothers' Keeper", is the churches' ministerial response to our youths' socio-economic, existential crises. It provides ministries that will preach the gospel to young males, heal their wounded spirit, and deliver them from drugs, violence and criminal behavior. "My Brothers' Keeper", is a manual on how to fight the substance abuse, gang activity, immorality and violence amongst our youth. It is a battle strategy that the church can use to break their spiritual, psychological and social chains. "My Brothers 'Keeper", provides information and the inspiration needed for the church to do effective ministry to young males and should be helpful for all pastors , deacons , church school teachers, youth workers , guidance counselors, social workers and everyone who cares about the welfare of our boys. "My Brothers' Keeper", is a handbook on how to liberate our young men, the laity and parents from existential bondage.

We are our brothers' keeper. It does not matter what your race, class, gender, or creed is. It does not matter if you are Christian, Muslim, Jewish, atheistic or humanistic. It should not matter if your political affiliation is Democrat, Republican, liberal, conservative, socialist or tea party. The only thing that should matter is that you are a part of the human family. Since we are all a part of the human family, we are responsible for one another. We are our brothers' keeper. We need each other. We must care for one another. We should love one another. We need to liberate one another. Each of us holds the key to the others freedom. If our youth are in bondage, then we are in bondage. If they are shackled to drugs, criminality and poverty, then we are not totally free. Once we set them free, we shall be free. Their freedom is our freedom. Moreover, the same God who set us free, can set them free.

There is nothing our God can't do and no one He can't liberate. If He can liberate Moses and the people of Israel from Egyptian bondage, He can liberate Americas' young men from social, psychological and spiritual bondage. God can save anybody, anytime from anything. I am a living witness to the grace of God. His grace saved my soul and granted me eternal life in His name. God literally delivered me from my narcissistic, hedonistic lifestyle to become saved, sanctified and filled with the Holy Ghost. He took me off the streets and into His pulpit. If God can deliver me, I know He can deliver anyone. My hopes for our young men is not based on any philosophy, theory, religion, political party, government program or church ministry but on the precious blood of Jesus Christ. The song writer was right, "My hope is built on nothing less than Jesus blood and righteousness. I dare not trust the sweetest frame, but wholly lean on Jesus name. On Christ the solid rock I stand, all other ground is sinking sand. On Christ the solid rock I stand, all other ground is sinking sand."

Introduction-End Notes

1   Denise Smith, "Big drug traffickers launder money; little guys spend it." The Detroit News, 15 July 1990, Sec. 8A.

2   Ibid.

Chapter One

Social Chains of Young African American Males

"A boy is born in hard time Mississippi surrounded by four walls that ain't too pretty. His parents give him love and affection to keep him strong moving in the right direction. Living just enough, just enough for the city." Stevie Wonder, Living for the City

"Man is born free; and everywhere he is in chains." Rousseau

Far too many young African American males are living for the city. They live in cities where there is a proliferation of crime, drugs, and violence. They live in deplorable, rat infested slums, attend substandard public schools and survive in urban blight. Every day they are exposed to drug dealing, criminal activities, homelessness, gangs, unemployment, prostitution and violence. Too many young African American males are victims of city living. The city has socially conditioned them for failure and fueled them with hopelessness and despair.

The social environment of some adolescent minority males shackle them to a life of crime, violence, sexual promiscuity, unemployment and substance abuse. The shackles of misery and mediocrity avert their ascendancy. Very few of them escape to experience life, liberty, and the pursuit of happiness. The vast majority of them are socially conditioned to live unproductive, self-destructive lives. The bible is right, "Do not be deceived: Bad company ruins good morals." (I. Corinthians 15:33) The Bad company, the gangs, poverty, crime and drug culture contributes to the bad behavior of our boys. So many of them have been shaped by their evil environment.

SOCIOLOGICAL PORTRAIT OF A CHURCH NEIGHBORHOOD

The church I pastored, was located in north- west Detroit, with a census of 189,588 people. It was predominantly African-American with single-parent families. Some of the homes had been abandoned and became crack houses. The area had suffered from racial transition. White owned businesses had left and the area was in need of commercial development. The neighborhoods were plagued by youth unemployment, gang violence, crack houses and high school dropouts. The area had extremely high burglaries and other criminal activity. There were two neighborhood high schools in the area. They both were known for high dropout rates. There is only one recreational facility in the area and it was overflowing with young people. The lack of community organizations for youth had a negative effect on them. Their restless energy was channeled in negative ways. Consequently adolescent African American males were seen loitering or wandering the streets vulnerable to criminal activity.

EMPIRICAL FINDINGS ABOUT CHURCH YOUTH

We conducted surveys and interviews on adolescent African American male church members and discovered their values. We wanted to ascertain how the social environment surrounding the church effected them. We believed that the only way to save our youth is to know them. In interviews, many of them struggled with being tempted to sell drugs, participate in gangs or engage in some criminal activity. They shared that they were under enormous pressure to join gangs and engage in criminal activity. Most of the youth were unemployed or underemployed. Those who worked part-time jobs were at fast food restaurants and grocery stores. Those who could not find a job were under a lot of pressure to engage in drug dealing or in scavenger gangs that engaged in illegal activity. There were small-time drug dealers who were a part of the congregation. Some of the boys drank and or got high on marijuana. Most of the boys had friends who were either in jail, been arrested, addicted to drugs, selling drugs or killed because of drugs.

In interviews and surveys it was discovered that the majority of youth didn't like school or spend a lot of time with their family. They felt that their teachers were too restrictive and not approachable. Similarly they believed that their parents or guardians were too strict and domineering. They had an anti-authoritarian posture that respected no one who had power over them. Most of the boys didn't have a job. Some worked in various service jobs. A couple of the members admitted that they acted as drug runners and were afraid of getting caught or killed. A majority of the boys didn't think that this country treated African-Americans fairly. They strongly believed that this nation was unjust to the poor and minorities. There was an overwhelming attitude of cynicism and skepticism about the local, state and federal governments. None of them had any interest in voting. They thought it was a waste of time. Many of the young people were angry at life in general and did not see a future for themselves. The majority of boys loved Rap music and some of them wanted to be entertainers. Most of the boys loved to play basketball and some aspired to be professionals. All of the boys did not like or trust the police. They had a "no snitch" policy that prohibited them from telling the police about criminal activity. Most of the boys did not know who their fathers were, did not have a good relationship with their fathers or have a positive male role model in their life. They had a love-hate relationship with women in their lives. They loved and admired their mothers but were disrespectful and demeaning to most women. They saw women as strippers to be sexually conquered.

UNEMPLOYMENT OF BLACK YOUTH

The African American male's predicament is primarily the result of economic and social factors. Institutional racism, decline of older manufacturing centers, structural constraints, the effects of nepotism, lack of training, and the political powerlessness of Blacks has led to the impoverishment and endangerment of young Black males. High African American male unemployment and underemployment can be attributed to a shift in economic activity from goods production to services, to a lack of adequate skills and training, and to racism in hiring practices. [2]

Many African American males are largely concentrated in inner cities that have experienced a decline in blue-collar employment and an expansion of "knowledge intensive" fields such as advertising, finance, brokering, accounting, and law. The rising unemployment rates among young Black males reflects the development of a class of workers who are confronted with prolonged and chronic unemployment and relegation as a permanent underclass. [3] Many African American males have not developed a skill set to address this shift to a" knowledge- intensive" job market. There are many analysts who believe that young Blacks are refusing to work at low-wage and manual labor jobs. [5]

Most of the adolescent males whom I interviewed never had a permanent job in their lives. Many of them shared with me that they would like to "own my own business one day." But none of them was willing to fulfill the necessary educational requirements to do so. One incarcerated 17-year-old youth told me," I will never work nine to five. My mama did that but not me. Besides what do I need to work at Mickey D's for little minimum-wage, when I can make hundred times that much in an hour? You got to be crazy to do that work." This adolescent was well aware of his limited employment opportunities. He knew that he could work only at a manual labor job for minimum wage. Instead he chose the highly lucrative drug trade over the lowly wages of a fast food restaurant. His social attitude typifies the African American adolescent. These adolescents are aware that they will never achieve the "American Dream" by flipping hamburgers. For them it is a mockery to believe that financial prosperity can be achieved with manual labor jobs. They have seen too many of their parents, guardians and relatives eke out a meager living. African American adolescents have observed how adults with full-time jobs and a diligent work ethic can still end up poor. [6] It is their social awareness of society's discriminatory practices that lead some adolescents to death at an early age. It is the psychological death of feeling inferior and of abusing drugs. It is a spiritual dissolution of resigning for life of despair, self-destructive behavior, and immorality. It is a social catastrophe of having been denied life, liberty, and the pursuit of happiness. It is because of the plight of African American adolescents that Jawanza Kunjufu calls them the "endangered species." [7]

The African American male is becoming an endangered species. The plight of the African American male has resulted in his having a shorter life expectancy, a greater unemployment and underemployment rate, a greater probability of being involved in violent crime, and a higher dropout rate than both his white and Black female counterparts. The probability of young Black males having a quality of life drastically inferior to that of their white counterparts is alarming: 86% of black youth live in poverty; between 46% and 52% are unemployed and one out of every six black males will be arrested by the time he reaches the age of nineteen. According to Kunjufu, African American males are victims of a cabal in American society. There is a complex conspiracy with those who promote drugs, gang violence, institutional racism, and a passive group of conspirators of parents, educators, and pseudo-liberals who allow the continued psychological, spiritual, and social death of Black boys. [9] Kunjufu's strong indictment of American society is understandable when looking at the systematic economic injustices suffered by African American males.

DRUGS AND ECONOMICS

The economic shifts that have taken place throughout United States have had an extremely detrimental effect on African American males. Sociologist William J. Wilson states that the relocation of many inner-city businesses to the suburbs, and Third World, are increasing unemployment rates among Black male population. Unskilled Black males are unable to find jobs and are disproportionately represented in blue-collar occupations. Wilson explains that traditional sources of employment are unavailable for Black males. Consequently, many central cities have become dangerous havens for drug trafficking and black males represent an unfortunate symbol of decline of the nation's cities. The Urban League stated that the unemployment of 25 to 44 year old Black males is two to four times higher than that of white males. The average white male's full-time weekly wages were twice as high as the average Black male. Furthermore, for Black male's youth the unemployment rate is about 35%. Today's Black males cannot attain the financial status of previous generations when their service jobs pay one- third less than most blue-collar jobs.

The Bureau of Labor Statistics stated that 58% of all future jobs require four years of high school and 1 to 2 years of college. Presently African Americans are heavily concentrated in certain low skill jobs and account for 54% of private home cleaners, nursing aides, and orderlies. Unemployment, underemployment and a lack of economic opportunities are some of the social economic factors that foster drug dealing. Society has discriminated against Black males and deprived them of the economic wherewithal to be "bread winners" in the home. Consequently, some of them have turned to the lucrative and dangerous drug trade. Dr. Hechman said, "Criminal activity is linked to opportunities in the mainstream economy… many participants in the underground economy are making sizable incomes… larger than they could have earned in the conventional economy."

CYCLE OF DESTITUTION, DRUGS AND DEATH

African American males can get caught in a vicious cycle unemployment, drugs and violence. This tragic cycle often ends with murder. There is a rapid increase in the homicide rate among African American males under the age of 40. The homicide rate is 10 times higher for black men than for white men. Homicide is the leading cause of death for African American Black males in the United States. There is a 1 in 21 life-time chance of being murdered. For white males, the chance is 1 in 131.

In Detroit, Michigan the cycle of destitution, drugs and death is very prevalent. Youth unemployment has led to a mass distribution of crack cocaine. Crack cocaine is a highly potent cocaine derivative that has devastated urban neighborhoods. Its primary victims and victimizers are adolescent African American males. Many have fought and died over the enormous amount of money and power of the drug trade. The involvement of Black males in the distribution of drugs is a primary way for them to achieve the" American dream". As one young drug runner confessed, "Hey I know it isn't right. But the money is good. I can get whatever I want when I want." Unfortunately many of them get death from a rival drug dealer or even a relative. This pastor will never forget the funeral I conducted for young male member who was shot in the head because of a drug deal that went bad. It was a tragic episode in the life of the church because the murderer and the victim were first cousins. There weren't any adequate words to comfort these grieving mothers and their families that were destroyed by the drug trade.

PUBLIC SCHOOL FAILURE

One of the reasons why public schools fail African American males is because of the institution's pedagogy. The domineering relationship between teacher and student can be detrimental to the spirit, mental acuity, and creativity of the student. [10] In his renowned work Pedagogy of the Oppressed, Friero points out how public school teachers deposit irrelevant information into passive receptacles. These students or receptacles are not taught to be critical thinkers and are not taught to question authority. African American adolescents are explicitly taught to be submissive and intellectually inert. [11] Friero writes about the detrimental results of our educational pedagogy. He writes, "Thus teaching becomes an act of depositing in which the students are the depositories and the teacher is the depositor. This is the' banking' concept of education in which the scope of action allowed to the students extends only as far as receiving, filing ,and storing the deposits. They do, it is true, and have the opportunity to become collectors of catalogs of things they store. But in the last analysis, it is men themselves who are filed away through the lack of creativity, transformation, and knowledge." This educational process has been detrimental to some people. It has made many passive entities adapt to the ways of the world. Many have become brainwashed and unable to think for themselves. They have lost their creativity and independent thinking. This is especially true of African American male adolescents. They are not only taught from a Eurocentric perspective that ignores or belittles the enormous achievements and contributions of African Americans but are trained to be what Eric Fromm calls an automaton--- a person who relies solely on the input instruction of others. [14] This has led to intellectual dissolution and broken spirit of millions of African American children. William Glasser's book, Schools Failure, states: "Smart children soon learn that what is important in school …We must teach students the relationships between what they are learning and their lives. Our failure to do so is a major cause of failure in school. Children discover that in school they must use their brains mostly for committing facts to memory rather than expressing their interests or ideas to solve problems. Increasingly, with each passing year thinking is less valuable than memorizing. Education does not emphasize thinking and is so memory oriented that almost all schools are dominated by the 'certainty principle.' According to the 'certainty principle' there are right and wrong answers to every question. The function of education is to ensure that each student knows the right answers to predetermined questions that educators have decided are important. As the certainty principle dominates our educational system, we will not teach our children to think. Memorizing is not knowledge. Certainty and memory are the enemies and destroyers of creativity and originality. It is no wonder, therefore, that memorization so prized in the current education and leads to boredom to those who are successful and frustration and misery for those who are not." [15]

The present educational system seems to be unable to meet the needs of African American males. Far too many public schools have produce low standardized test scores, a lack of problem solving skills, negative work attitudes and a poor foundation for continuous learning. Moreover, some of the public schools have textbooks that are outdated, tattered and Eurocentric. Some of the teachers are over worked, underpaid and out of touch with Black youth culture. There is apathy among students, teachers, parents and administrators. When I visited a local public school, I was appalled by the chaos and confusion of the classroom. I saw African-American students fighting and arguing with each other. I witnessed complacent and apathetic teachers who seemed more interested in watching the clock than teaching their students. I saw students that appeared to be high or drunk. I even think I saw money being exchanged for drugs. The schools were more like a warehouse than an educational institution.

INTELLECTUAL DEATH AT AN EARLY AGE

It is no wonder that many African American students drop out of school. It is no surprise that many African American youth end up in prison, strung out on crack, murdered or dealing drugs. When and how do the public schools fail them? It can be argued that our public schools miseducation and disincline African American males at a very early age. The innocence and enthusiasm for learning is stripped from them as early as second grade. In primary schools, African American males are indoctrinated in a Eurocentric curriculum, emasculated by some female teachers and brainwashed to believe they are inferior. Morgan delineates in his book, How Schools Fail Black Children, "When Blacks enter first-grade they express positive feelings about themselves in the schooling but by second grade students express negative imagery of the teacher and school and by fifth grade the overall feeling expressed by students is that cynicism. In other words upon entering school in primary grades, Black children possess enthusiasm and eager interest; however, by fifth grade the liveliness and interests are replaced by passivity and apathy. Primary grades presented a more nurturing environment than the intermediate or upper grades. In early childhood education much of the activity is child-teacher centered and child-child interactive. In primary grades, Blacks progress and thrive at the same rate as their White counterparts until the third grade syndrome. I found after the third grade achievement rate of blacks began a downward spiral which tended to continue in the child's academic career. Classroom environment was transformed from a socially interactive style to a competitive, individualistic and minimally socially interactive style of learning." [16]

The downward spiral of academic excellence among African American males accelerates in high school. The dropout rates among black males is appallingly high and continues to increase. A high school dropout doesn't have the formal training necessary to achieve in life. He has relegated himself to a lower lifetime earnings. A high school dropout who refuses to return get his GED resigns himself to a life of poverty and powerlessness. Jewell Gibbs expresses how Black male dropouts are especially vulnerable." The high dropout rates of 18 and 19 year old black males point to the importance of lowered potential earnings and the lack of credentials necessary for upward educational and economic mobility. Thus the ability of Black males who drop out of high school to provide for the basic needs, some of the advantages beyond this level, to families that many of them either desire to head becomes problematic." [17]

PUBLIC SCHOOLS MORAL FAILURE

One of the major failures of our public schools is that they don't require youth to attend classes in conflict resolution and moral/ ethical behavior. Some schools do offer classes of that nature. But the vast majority of public schools do not instruct our children and youth in how to live a peaceful, moral life. I am not suggesting that our public schools teach religion or become Christian. It is the role of the church to offer Christian education and religious training. But our public schools can and should require our youth to participate in conflict resolution and moral/ethics classes. Our youth should learn anger management, communication skills, conflict resolution and moral/ethical decision making. This will stem all of the fighting in and out of the classroom. They will learn how their moral-ethical behavior has social consequences. All of this can be taught without proselytizing and any references to any particular religion. Our children and youth can learn how to be good law-abiding citizens and live nonviolently.

One could argue that it is not the responsibility for Public schools to teach nonviolence and morals. Some would say it is the parent(s) or the churches responsibility to teach these issues and they are right. But the fact of the matter is, all of our families and our churches are not teaching these classes. Furthermore many families breed trouble makers and do not send their youth to church. Moreover many churches do not teach their youth conflict resolution courses. They may learn about Jesus but they haven't learned how to apply his biblical principles of nonviolence. It is because our public schools don't teach nonviolence that there is so much youth violence. The gang violence and mass killings like Columbine High School will continue, if the public schools don't teach nonviolence. Our youth will continue to have children out of wedlock and be substance abusers, if the public schools don't instruct them on morals/ethic. We must realize that we are in a crises and this crises demands fundamental changes in how and what we teach our youth. It will take more than bringing prayer back in the class room to change our youth. What good is it if a child can pray in the classroom when there is violence in the heart? What good is it if the child can pray in school but fights outside the school? It is time for our Federal government to provide the resources so that our public schools can adequately teach nonviolence and moral/ethics. If we are genuine about ending the chaos and carnage in the streets we must get our Public Schools involved teaching mandatory classes on conflict resolution, anger management, communication skills and morals/ethics.

DROP OUT OF SCHOOL TO DROP INTO DRUG CULTURE

When some African American males drop out of public school, they are generally educated by the drug culture. Lack of achievement and social discrimination are connected to the degree of drug involvement. Jewell Gibbs states: "Both educational attainment and current school enrollment showed an inverse relationship to degree of drug involvement: the last drug the more likely currently to be in school, to have completed and to aspire to higher educational levels. Half of those who had not used an illicit substance 51% were in school, either as their sole activity or in combination with working or looking for work. [18] The drug civilization was created by political leaders, corporate powerbrokers, bankers, and members of organized crime who profit by flying, shipping and smuggling hundreds of tons of drugs into our beloved country. The drug culture is a system of complicated bureaucratization as seen in today's corporate America. This type of bureaucratization to a drug dealer is known as the drug network.

DRUG EMPLOYER

The CEO of this drug network is referred to in the streets as an "employer". They are middle level dealers who are older males between the ages of 27 and 35. These dealers usually inhabit different neighborhoods than the ones they are selling drugs to. These middleman are rarely seen on street corners where their drugs are sold. An employer in the drug network exercise great influence over members of a network through their control over the source of the drugs. Also these people would usually employ 15 to 20 people on a regular basis. Most drug dealers rarely use drugs and perceived themselves as businessmen. Many drug dealers own legitimate businesses to conceal their drug trade .They own car washes, party stores, pages stores and beauty shops. These establishments are fronts to keep the IRS from investigating and police officers from suspecting them of criminal activity. Many of the drug dealer's wear expensive clothing, gaudy jewelry and drive expensive cars.

DRUG ENTREPRENEUR

The second highest position in a drug network is the vice president or the drug entrepreneur. These entrepreneurs are round ages 19 to 24. They do most of their business on street corners. Most do not hold legitimate jobs or attend school and they reside in the homes of their parents who exercise no control over them. Entrepreneurs have been able to bypass the middle level employers to establish the own independent connections with suppliers outside the community where they can obtain drugs directly in a relatively large amounts. They are solely responsible for safely transporting and storing the drug in the vicinity.

THE DRUG RIDER

The third highest position in a drug network is the "rider". These "riders" are round ages 17 to 20 years. Usually they live with their parents or relatives who exert some control over their behavior. Riders can earn a week wages in a day. Employers expect to be on the street corner on a regular basis. These people have exclusive relationships with their employer.

THE DRUG RUNNER

Runners make up another branch of the drug network. Runners differ from riders in that they do not have an exclusive relationship with the employer. They are around the ages 9 to 17 years. Usually runners live with parents who try to monitor their behavior. They consider selling drugs as a quick and easy way to make limited amount of money for recreational needs. For example they sell drugs when they want to purchase clothes, sneaker, video games, jewelry etc. The drug runner is schooled by drug dealers and becomes extremely street smart. Through on-the-job training they learn how to identify undercover cops and sell drugs with unsurpassed skill. Some of them are drug abusers and work to get high. Others are motivated by quick money and excitement. All drug runners are very loyal to the dealer for fear of their lives and financial security. Also there is a bonding between the dealer and runner that fulfills the paternal deprivation of the runner. Dealer acts as a Street Mentor for the runner and may set him up to be a dealer. The drug runner patiently waits on street for customer drive up to him and ask him for drugs. The drug runner has the drugs on him. Sometimes he hides it in inconspicuous places. After the runner has determined that the purchaser is not a police officer, he retrieves the drugs, sells them to the buyer. But he must be extremely knowledgeable so that he doesn't get caught by police or rival dealers. This street knowledge is gained through raw experience.

The tragic life of a nine-year old member and drug runner is an excellent example of the drug culture. This young man stopped going to school because it was boring. He never knew his father and was raised by a drug dependent mother. The dilapidated apartment that he lived in was located in an impoverished, drug infested neighborhood. He shared with me his life as a drug runner. He said he met a drug dealer when he was playing basketball. The dealer asked him to work for him as a drug runner. As a drug runner, he received the drugs from the drug dealer and gave them to the abuser. He then took the money back to the drug dealer from minimum charge. He was young enough to expose his peers to drugs and not old enough to go to jail. His drug dealer trained him to be swift, courageous, cunning carrier. He couldn't be afraid of the police, abusers and other drug dealers. He was skilled at being as inconspicuous as possible at every drug transaction. He was streetwise in getting in and out of difficult situations and extremely loyal and obedient to his employer. Insubordination, stealing and tardiness were not tolerated. He told me that if he did not do his job, it may mean a broken limb, roughing up and even death.

Another drug runner was lured into the trade by $20 bill. He told me that he was asked to drop off a small bag at a house around the corner from his apartment building. Ever since, he's been delivering drugs to his friends, adults and even his mother. He told me he admired his employer and liked the money he was receiving. He made a lot of money. He confessed to me that he was able to buy just about anything he wanted. He said he owns several pair of sneakers, some gold chains and some new clothes. I asked him about his future plans and if he would go back to school. He replied, "Why should I? I probably got more money than you. Besides so long as I'm working for my man I know I'll be straight." Street education, financing and sense of male bonding that he received from his drug dealer is representative of many African American adolescent male drug dealers. Unfortunately there are thousands like him born in urban poverty, dropped out of public school, and enter the drug culture. Even though their names and faces are different their biographies are similar. They all share similar training and drug trafficking and street sales. They learn how to purchase, cut and sell drugs. They discover how to make deals, how to handle the police, and how to manipulate their parents and the criminal justice system. If they are successful drug runners, they will receive financial and material rewards. They earn a lot of money, buy video games, jewelry, clothes and expensive designer sneakers. Some of them are given drugs and work to fulfill their addictions. The drug dealer instructs the runner with all he knows about the drug trade. If the drug runner remains faithful, he will matriculate to becoming a smalltime drug dealer or drug rider.

It is a sin against Almighty God for these young boys to sell drugs and be a part of an evil institution that is systematically destroying their lives, enslaving their souls and fragmenting their families. These boys must repent of their sins for selling poison to the community. They are literally killing people every day. They are guilty of murdering the masses. These dealers in death must repent before God or they will be eternally condemned. The bible is right, "The wages of sin is death and the gift of God is eternal life through Jesus Christ our Lord." We pray that God will use His courageous people to preach the gospel to them and they will be saved.

PEER GROUP AND GANGS

Another social factor that foster substance abuse among adolescent African American males is their peer group and gangs. During adolescence, one of their primary pressures is the peer group. Generally teachers, parents and clergy to do not have the impact on adolescents that their peers have. The adolescent sense of identity, values and behavior is developed by peer groups. [19] Peer groups give adolescents a sense of belonging, security, self-expression and self-esteem. [20] Peer groups socialize the African-American adolescents in the ways of the world. The peer group is a street institution that indoctrinate African American adolescents on ghetto colony. [21] "The streets constitute an institution in the same way that the church, school and family are conceived as institutions. They all have a set of values and norms to govern and reinforce their existence. Of course the social structure of the street lacks the sophistication these other institutions have. Nevertheless it is an institution because it helps to shape and control behavior. And it is on the streets where black child receives his basic orientation to life. The streets become his primary reference to cope with other institutions that have failed to provide him essential skills he needs to survive in the ghetto colony. He must undergo a rigorous apprenticeship that will enable him to compensate for the lack of guidance from other institutions and adults. He becomes a student of the asphalt jungle because that is where he can learn the skills he needs." [22]

It is truly a miracle that African American males can survive in a violent, hostile, poverty-stricken world. A world that attempts to break their spirits, strip them of their manhood and brainwash their minds. They are living in a situation that demands the strongest of faith, the deepest wells of the wisdom and the acuity of Einstein. What is amazing is that in spite of all the odds and obstacles they are able to eke out an existence. Praise God for all those parents who were able to raise good, strong, responsible, law-abiding Black men. We should especially recognize single mothers for the resiliency and tenacity. In spite of all the social hurdles they were able to teach their sons to not only survive but succeed. If it was not for strong single mothers we would not have a Frederick Douglass , James Brown , Stevie Wonder, Rev. Al Sharpton or President Barak Obama and many, many others.

Unfortunately there are parents that were not so successful. In spite of all their efforts they unwittingly raised drug dealers, gangsters, drug addicts and social deviants. One of the ways they are able to survive is through urban gangs of what today's youth call posse or crew. Dr. Taylor's, "Dangerous Society" states, "Gangs may be primarily defined within three different motivational categories scavenger, territorial and corporate." [23]

SCAVENGER GANGS

Scavenger Gangs have an informal, non-obligatory commitment to one another. Leadership and membership changes are frequent. Scavenger gangs don't have any particular goal, other than to engage in spontaneous, senseless theft, violence and reckless behavior. [24] One of the members of my church belonged to a scavenger gang. He was a descent young man who was 14 years old. I only saw him loitering on the streets with five other adolescence. I asked him why he stayed with them and what they did. He said, "Well, Rev. these fellas are my crew. They watch me and I watch them. Sometimes we play ball or check out some girls, or smoke some pot. But we don't do nothing wrong. You know we just hang. Every now and then we may choose someone for some money but it ain't like we are thugs or anything. We just get some money to eat and hang out." This young man needed to be saved from the scavenger gangs and needed the church to reach out to him.

TERRITORIAL GANGS

Another peer group that socializes young African American males is the Territorial gangs. This kind of gang emphasizes certain part of the neighborhood and boys belong exclusively to the gang. [25] In Territorial gangs, leaders and territory are clearly defined. They control the streets by violence and intimidation. They will attempt a put fear in the hearts of residents to enforce their territorial law. Their primary objective is to protect, preserve and prosper their dope houses. [26] Territorial gangs use physical violence to intimidate or even kill competitive rival gangs. They punish any outsiders that may trespass on their territorial boundaries and threaten their financial power. [27] Sometimes innocent bystanders are killed in rival gang wars. There are hundreds of casualties related to territorial wars. Children are shot, maimed and killed too frequently on the streets of Detroit because of territorial turf wars.

These gangs are terrorist organizations that are not only destroying our boys but also our society. They create so much terror on the streets that most urbanites are locked in our homes. The drive by shootings, gang wars, the gun shots and the killing makes living in the city feel like a war zone. The level of violence and bloodshed is unacceptable before our God. Our just and righteous God condemned the city of Nineveh because of its violence. Surely our God would do the same to our cities. All of the violence, murder, chaos and carnage in our cities is abhorrent to God. We might have become accustomed to it but God is not. He is disgusted by all of the hatred and hostility emitting from these gangs. His eternal truth still speaks to us, "He that lives by the sword, dies by the sword."

SOCIOECONOMIC FACTORS AND IMPLEMENTATION OF CHURCH MINISTRY

The information in Chapter one will be a used in training sessions for the laity. The training sessions will instruct the laity about the inadequate education of the public school system, the drug culture, peer and gang influences, high black unemployment, and high dropout rates that all lead to economic and social slavery. The implementation of the church ministry upon adolescent African American males will address joblessness, gang violence, and failure of public schools, drug culture and criminalization of youth. It is these social factors that lead black boys into social slavery.

Therefore the social factors experienced by Black boys must be addressed in the churches ministry to them. Since public schools do not teach conflict resolution, African American history or self-esteem the church must teach them. This will raise their self-esteem, their ability to resolve conflict and enhance their social mobility. Gangs and peers teach our Black Boys how to be violent and engage in criminal activity. The church can address this problem with a Christian Mentoring program that will develop boys into men. Some of the principles in the Rites of passage will inspire the juvenile's to create their own jobs through conscientious legitimate creative means. The Rites of Passage will give the boys a more positive peer group that will lead to a moral socialization process. There can be weekly group discussions that can teach biblical principles within youth culture. Moreover, the laity will instruct them on how to manage their anger and conflict.

Chapter One-End Notes

1   Jewell Young, Black and Male in, p.119.
2   William, The Truly Disadvantaged: The Inner City, the Underclass, and Public Policy (Univ. of Chicago, 1987) 100-102.
3   Gibbs, p. 103.
4   Ibid., pp.100-102.
5   p.102
6   Jawanza Kunjufu, Developing Positive Self-Image and Disciplines in Black Children, Chicago, IL, 1984, p.32.
7   vii.
8   Kenneth M. Jones, "The Black Male in Jeopardy," The Crises, Vol. 93, #3, March 1986: 27, 28.
9   p.1.
10 Ibid.
11 Ibid. p.33.
12 Paula Friero, Pedagogy of the Oppressed, NY Continuum, 1970, pp. 59-63.
13 Kunjufu, p.34.
14 Eric Fromm, Escape from Freedom, Discus Books, New York, 1972, p.18.
15 Alvin Poussaint, "Building a Strong Self-Image in Black Children," Ebony Magazine, August 1974, pp.138-143.
16 Gibbs, pp. 176-177.
17 Harry Morgan, "How Schools Fail Black Children," Social Policy, Jan-Feb, 1980, pp.49-54.
18 Gibbs, pp.176-177.
19 Sampson, p.17.
20 Ibid. p. 18.
21 Jawanza Kunjufu, Countering the Conspiracy to Destroy Black Boys, p. 14.
22 Ibid.
23 Carl S. Taylor, Dangerous Society, Mich. State Univ. Press, East Lansing, MI, 1990,p.4.
24 Ibid.
25 Ibid.p.6.
26 Ibid.
27 Ibid.

Chapter Two

Psychological Chains of Young African American Males

"Pride cometh before destruction, a haughty spirit
before the fall." (Proverbs 16:18)

"What do you got coming to you? The world Chico…and everything in it." The movie, SCARFACE

The psyche of the adolescent African American male drug dealer has been shaped by an identity crisis, paternal deprivation, and negative socialization process which has given him an inferiority complex. His low self-worth has led him to engage in acts of self-glorification. He may look and act like a phlegmatic King, but underneath the glitter and gold is a bellicose boy who feels worthless and insignificant. His twisted mentality compels him to do whatever is incumbent to feel preeminently majestic. His emptiness and shallowness drive him to be a conspicuous consumer, subjugator of those he considers his inferiors, drug abuser, and unrestrainable ruffian. Some of these adolescent African American drug dealers admire and emulate the movie icon Scarface. They hustle, lie, cheat, steal and kill to be powerful, prosperous drug dealers.

PSYCHE OF CHURCH YOUTH

A similar statement can be said of the non-drug dealing adolescent African American males of the church. They are boys struggling with an identity crisis and an inferiority complex. Consequently for them manhood means using drugs, being sexually promiscuous, arrogant, hostile and materialistic. Through surveys, essays and interviews with adolescent African American males within the church and surrounding community we were able to assess their self-perceptions, feelings and behavior. This was used to inform the laity about the psyche of black males and create a church program that would address their psychological needs.

In interviews and surveys of ex-drug dealers, drug users and adolescent African American males we discovered that most of them had a very poor self - image and lacked self-esteem. Many of them said they did not feel good about themselves. Some talked about feeling a sense of futility and despair about life. They felt like failures at home and in school. Our survey revealed that the majority of adolescent African American males were raised solely by their mothers and had an identity crisis. Most of them felt a great deal of love for their mothers and anger or ambivalence for their absent fathers. More than three-fourths of the youth experience nonfulfillment in their home. There domestic situation made them feel inadequate and inferior at times. As one young man stated," I never feel like I'm doing enough. Even when I'm home, I'm not at home."

Another survey revealed their feelings of failure at school. More than 90% of the high school youth surveyed were doing no better than a D average. The majority of them admitted that they were doing really poorly in school. Most of them believed that the teachers didn't really care about them and were going through the motions. Almost all of them didn't appreciate the relevance of going to school. Seventy-five percent of the boys thought about dropping out of school early. All of them felt inept at studying and academically inferior.

Some incarcerated young African American males were asked to write essays about how they felt as ex drug dealers or runners. The essays revealed that many of them felt like" kings" of the city. They were able to amass small fortunes, drive expensive cars, wear the latest attire, and influence a lot of people. They felt they were revered by peers, feared by elderly, and loved by women. Some of them said selling drugs made them feel like somebody special and when they weren't selling drugs they felt worthless. For many of them drug dealing and buying superfluous material possessions was an attempt to compensate for their lack of self-worth. They were really concealing a deep inferiority complex and they were desperately in need of affirmation.

All of them stated that the principal motivation for selling drugs was money and material possessions. Some of them believed they were no different from the average businessman. They were not concerned about the welfare of the drug addicts, the community or themselves. Their primary concern was making as much money as possible. Many of the ex-drug dealers stated they missed all the money they had. Some said they doubted they could do a 9 to 5 job earning minimum wage. They had gotten accustomed to having a high standard of living. The majority of adolescents admired drug dealers and wanted to be like them. Some ex drug dealers had a strong positive advice to give young people about drugs. They would tell their peers that all of the wealth and materialism wasn't worth endangering one's life. They loved the treasures and pleasures of the world, but hated illegal consequences. Some of the young males did not feel free enough to express their true feelings and thoughts. There was a feeling of being a "cage bird" that is trapped by society and within. Their sense of imprisonment is accompanied by an acute anger focused on society and themselves. Anger seems to be the overriding emotion for most black male adolescents who were products of dysfunctional families. Family conflicts, abusive parents, drug abuse had produced deviant, violent young men.

The principal psychological factors that contribute to substance abuse among adolescent African American males are an identity crisis, lack of positive male role models, and a low self-esteem. This information is critical to the training of the lay team for ministry. The more the laity know about mindset of African American males the more equipped they will be to be mentors, counselors and youth workers.

PSYCHOLOGICAL CHARACTERISTICS OF ADOLESCENTS

Adolescence entails the time between our childhood and adulthood. It is generally considered to begin at about 12 and concludes at around 20 years old. Adolescence is a time of physiological, psychological change that affects social behavior. Those experiencing adolescence begin to form an ego identity that utilizes cultural, historical and personal elements. They begin to develop their own ideas, attitudes, and interests. Their identity is beginning to emerge.

Jean Piaget delineates the characteristics of adolescent cognitive development.

1. Deal with the problems in which several factors operate simultaneously.
2. Utilize a multiple symbol system.
3. Construct ideal situations, a premise, and related argumentation.
4. Deal with the future as a norm of reality.
5. Grasp and develop alternative to parental directives.
6. Think introspectively, from the perspective of others. Adolescent self-consciousness is an indication of the capacity for introspection.
7. Determine that thoughts are private and personal.
8. Determine moral and just evaluations on society, family life, adult practices, modes of integrity, and religion based upon his capacity to construct the ideal condition. [2]

Piaget enables us to understand the self-centeredness, moodiness, and identity crisis of the adolescent. The adolescent is really struggling for identity in relation to his peers, society and family. He is trying to evaluate himself and discover who he is. Adolescents are searching for meaning and purpose in life. He is constantly shifting and editing his beliefs. It is a time of transition and self-discovery. He begins to have doubts about everything and everyone. This is largely because:

1. The failure of present information and experience harmonize with previously accepted beliefs and teachings.

2. The mere opportunity, felt freedom, independence, and new ability to evaluate, contrast, make decisions, and handle the enterprise of life from his vastly increased mental resource.

3. The physical changes in his body force assessment of self in relationship to the world and people around him. The sexual drive becomes a new factor in his negotiations with the world.

4. A sense of purity and moral simplicity leads to closer scrutiny of the world. [3]

The identity crisis experienced by all adolescence is even more acute within the African American male experience. The adolescent African American male struggles with his racial and male identity. Society has socialized him to believe that his race and manhood is inferior. Negative stereotypes of African Americans in literature, media, education systems and social customs have a detrimental effect on the African American adolescent. He develops an inferiority complex that reflects his socialization process.[4]

IDENTITY CRISES

One of the disturbing problems I see in African American adolescents at the church, is their identity crisis. Many of the young men interviewed did not think much of themselves. Most of them thought of themselves and others in racially derogatory terms .They did not think of themselves as being productive, successful young men with a bright, promising future. They perceived themselves as ignorant, unproductive, "n" with no future. The only profession they believed they could aspire to be was a drug dealer, a professional athlete or Rapper. Few believe that they could become doctors, lawyers, businessmen or other professionals. These adolescents essentially perceived themselves as "nobodies". When I asked them," How do you become a man?" The vast majority of them responded," by having a baby." For them sexual activity and procreation determined manhood. They did not realize that any boy can have a baby. But it takes a man to raise a child. Unfortunately, they placed a high premium on their physical attributes not their character or mental abilities. There negative self-image was largely due to a racist socialization process. There psychologically debilitating experiences in society had a profound impact creating a negative self- perception. Consequently they developed a low self-esteem that manifested itself in self-destructive behavior. The wearing sagging pants ,substance abuse , using racially derogatory names ,poor grades, dropping out of school, participating in gangs , acting as a bully , being disrespectful to others , sexual promiscuity, apathy, lack of a morality and slave mentality are all symptoms of a poor self-esteem. They have unconsciously fulfilled the stereotypes that society has ascribed to them. Their negative self-esteem was developed by a racist socialization process. [5] The" looking glass" that Black adolescents observe creates a low self-esteem. Self-esteem is the process by which we perceive ourselves. It is our sense of identity and images of ourselves.

Unfortunately, many young Black males do not realize that God loves them and wants them to love themselves. It is Gods will that young Black males not refer to themselves or others in racially derogatory terms. They must begin to see themselves as God sees them. God sees them as his children who are marvelously and fearfully made. They must begin to base their self-esteem on the grace of God and His son Jesus Christ. It is through Christ that they become "new creatures" made in the image of God. It is their divine identity in Christ that will bolster their low self-esteem and enable them to overcome the discrimination and dehumanization of the world.

BLACK SELF ESTEEM

Black self-esteem is how African American males see themselves. Our self- perception can reflect positive or negative self- images. A positive self- image can produce a healthy, adjusted personality and a negative self- image can create a maladjusted personality that is withdrawn, and feels worthless. It may lead to self-destructive behavior. There are glaring differences between those with a low self-esteem and a strong self-esteem. The characteristics of those who have a healthy self-esteem are as follows:

1. A self-performance rating and resulting discrepancies, seen in the light of assimilated standards and personal talents and abilities.
2. A history of successes and failures in meaningful goals and enterprises particularly within peer group relationships.
3. The ability and opportunity to have full self- expression within the individuals' desired sphere of activity.
4. The ability to handle difficult behavior situations and problems encountered within a certain group.
5. A feeling of autonomy, confidence, and independence within the group.
6. The felt approval and assurance generated by responsible persons, such as parents and teachers.
7. They perceived general status of ones' sound class and ethnic group rather than mere numbers in the group.
8. The occupation of the parents and the perceived social status of the family. [6]

Persons with low self- esteem have the following characteristics:

1. Withdraw from other people.
2. Feel that their opinions and possible contributions are not worth stating.
3. Feel that they are not able to affect the groups' action, to which they belong
4. Hesitate from moving to accomplish their goals and aspirations.
5. Accept and challenge questionable actions and opinions of others. They are more willing to conform to group persuasions, authority figures, and strong personalities.
6. Experience more frequent and intense anxieties, and are less able to cope with diverse situations.
7. Underestimate their own success, and overstress their own failures. They have difficulty resisting negative self-appraisals.
8. Feel greater anxiety about negative qualities involving family and primary relationships.
9. Hold less optimistic expectations of the future.
10. Feel more powerless about life and circumstances in general.

11. Have less success in school and in learning productivity. [7]

In the many different interviews that we have conducted, a low self-esteem was common among the young African American male. The greatest expression of their low self-esteem was their participation in the drug culture. In interviews with the boys we discovered that they had no dreams of the future. The boys did not feel that they could do anything about their future. They expressed feelings of hopelessness and despair. Their low self-esteem made it hard for them to believe in themselves. All of our interviewees had a very poor self- image, felt alienated from their family, the church and the community. One drug dealer confessed," I never was any good school. I am not book smart you know. But I know how to roll." This young man dropped out of school at the tender age of 14 and never returned. He felt intellectually inferior in an academic setting. He was proud that he could make money on the street selling drugs. But it was his poor self-esteem that made them drop out of school, fall into the drug trade and stay in it.

There was a 17-year-old who sold crack cocaine. In my conversations with him, he shared his sense of hopelessness and futility. He told me, "You know I really don't think I'm going to live to be old and gray. I been shot twice and been in jail a couple of times. You know if the "man" don't get me some punk will." His sense of futility and refusing to get out of the drug trade revealed his low self-esteem. I tried to encourage him to go back to get his GED but he refused saying, "There's no money in it. There's no future in that stuff." He had a low self-esteem that led him to live a reckless, deadly lifestyle. For him and other young men, their low self-esteem contributed to their use and distribution of drugs. Many young men pretended to be confident but hid their "toxic shame". [8]

According to John Bradshaw, Toxic shame is the rupture of the self and an innate feeling of unworthiness. Some expressed it in self-defeating attitude. They are unwilling to strive beyond the levels of mediocrity. Others think very little of themselves and will project a false self or image. They feel so flawed and defective that they pretend to be something that they are not. The young African American drug dealer is a prime example of someone who has toxic shame.

Carl Jung would say the African American drug dealer uses a persona or mask. Robert Stubby writes how people feel so inferior that they use a public self over against their private self which is the true essence of themselves. The Transactional Analysis speak of this false self as the "Adaptive child." This false self is a facade used to conceal deep feelings of inferiority and shame. It can be argued that the swagger, gaudy gold chains, the bragging, the ostentatious dress and the luxurious lifestyle of the African American male is a manifestation of his false self. It is his way of telling himself and the world that he is somebody. It can be argued that the acquisition of such embellishments can create a sense of self-worth and personal empowerment. But the easy money and materialism is a distorted perverted version of the American Dream. Underneath the gold and glitter is a morally corrupt soul.

I once knew a 24-year-old drug dealer who proudly showed off his beautiful Mercedes Benz, Cadillac Escalade and Lamborghini. He would brag about all the money he made, women he had and property he owned. He enjoyed talking about himself and his ability to make thousands of dollars. He drove luxury automobiles that concealed his toxic shame. He admitted that he felt ashamed for not graduating out of high school. He once confessed." You know one day I may go back and get my GED. I want to be able to teach my baby girl how to do math, read and write. My baby girl asked me a math question the other day and I played it off. I told her to ask her mama. Man I didn't know what it was." As self-assured and arrogant as he was, he could be stripped of his public image by his little daughter's simple math question. He typifies the shame-based personality of the African American drug dealer that manifest itself in gross materialism and braggadocios behavior. They have been socialized to believe that they can never achieve anything in life and won't ever become anything. This sense of shame is internalized and creates a deep inferiority complex. As a result of the inner pain the private self is abandoned and is lost to the public self that is expressed in gross materialism. African American male drug dealers are the most alienated men in society. He is estranged from himself, family, community and God.

The young drug dealer is liken to the rich man in the parable of building bigger barns. In the parable the rich farmer kept building bigger barns to store the overabundance of his crops. He was so inflated with pride and prosperity that he didn't think of God or anyone else. Then God visited him and said, "You Fool! This very night your life is being demanded of you. And the things you have prepared, whose will they be." Luke 12:20 The rich drug dealer amasses all of his property, possessions, cars, homes, and jewelry and thinks nothing of it. He doesn't realize that all of his material acquisitions that he received through his illegal activities will not shield him from the judgment of God.

FATHER ABSENT HOMES

Another psychological factor that negatively affects the African American male psyche is the emotional or physical absence of their fathers. [9] According to 2012 Whitehouse Fatherhood Report one out of every three children in America – more than 24 million in total- live in a home without their biological father present. Roughly one out of every three Hispanic children and more than half of African American children also live in homes without biological fathers. African American males have been deprived of having fathers or positive male role models. Society has economically and politically emasculated the African American males. His inability to provide for his family has affected his sons' psyche. There are very few strong father images in the black community. The African American male's inability to fulfill his traditional social role as the primary provider for his family results in his lacking self-esteem and experiencing rage and frustration. These feelings manifest themselves in aggression, which may sometime result in his being involved in serious criminal activities. Forty-five percent of Americans arrested for murder were African American. [11] In addition, the Black male may participate in illegal economic activities i.e. drug dealing in order to compensate for his unemployment, underemployment. Twenty-five percent of the income of Black youth comes from crime. [12]

The current plight of adult African American males affects the future of their adolescence sons' negatively. African American boys are being raised in "fatherless" homes and in crime infested neighborhoods. So their immediate environment fails to provide them with an adequate number of positive African American male role models. [13] Consequently, many African American adolescents imitate bad role models in their environment. Many of their role models have no education, have criminal records, part of the drug network, members of street gangs or who have menial or service occupations. [14]

WOUNDED FATHER

Moreover, many African American adolescent role models are drug dealers, addicts and criminals. Most of the adolescents that I interviewed did not have a father in their home. Their fathers were either incarcerated, abandoned the family, divorced, murdered or substance abusers. The few that had fathers physically present were emotionally absent. Their fathers were occupied with their jobs. Some of them were psychologically abusive. Dr. Samuel Osherson, states all men have a "wounded father" within which represents our psychological and emotional brokenness. Men have been internally ruptured by the lack of relationship with their fathers. They have been deprived of a sense of stability, and security from their fathers. Their paternal deprivation leads men to fulfill their father hunger and mentoring relationships. [15] Unfortunately the mentors for young African American males are drug dealers, gangsters and substance abusers. These malevolent mentoring relationships are bringing about the social and moral destruction of the community. The bible is right, "Bad companions make bad behavior." Criminalized youth are raising, nurturing, teaching and mentoring youth to be criminals.

Fatherhood is a sacred and special role for men. Fathers are not only required to care for their children's material welfare but also their spiritual welfare. It is the father's role to be a spiritual example for their children and teach them the word of God. It is the father's role to lead their sons to a saving knowledge of Jesus Christ, help them become men. (Deuteronomy 4:9-10;

11:19) There is no excuse for a man not to take care of his children. Mean-spirited ex –wives, disgruntled girlfriends, personal vices, blended families, unemployment, lack of paternal experiences, past issues, demanding job, pursuing a career, attending school are poor excuses for not taking care of your children. There is no excuse for fathers not to spend quality time with their sons. It's the father's moral mandate to raise, nature, teach and train his son in the paths of righteousness. Fathers should not let any street thug or drug dealer mentor their sons. The bible says, "He who will not take care of his own household is worse than an infidel." The worse thing any man could do is abandon, neglect or reject his own flesh and blood. A man who will not take care of his children is no man. It takes a real man to raise a son into manhood. Any man who is an absentee father is by default raising a drug dealer, gangster, car jacker, drug addict or criminal. Absentee fathers are partly responsible for the crime and violence that is permeating our community. They have unconsciously raised angry, alienated, hostile African American boys that are terrorizing our neighborhood. The rage and violence these boys have stems from their broken relationship with their fathers. The bible warns us, "Fathers, do no provoke your children to anger, but bring them up in the discipline and instruction of the Lord." (Ephesians 6:4) Fathers must repent of provoking the anger and rage in their sons. They must spend more quality time with their sons teaching them about the Lord.

FAMILY VIOLENCE AND YOUTH GANGS: PSYCHOLOGY

The family morals, values and beliefs are extremely critical issues in the development of violence in gangs. Violent behavior by juveniles against members of their own family is a topic which is only recently received attention. A nationwide Department of Justice (1980) revealed an estimated 1.2 million violent occurrences among relatives. Family conflicts and quarrels were found to be the major reasons for violence and 70% of this violence occurred in and around the home. Of the 1.2 million cases, seventy-four thousand involved parental violence against children, and forty seven thousand involved a child's violence towards parents. [16] Wolfgang and Ferracuti (1067) argued that overt expression of violence are part of the norms for the lower socio- economic classes and are learned responses to the pressures of survival. [17] Juvenile violence, according to this theory, can be explained by the fact that young males, and particularly in female-headed households in black or lower class areas are frustrated in their search for material goods, dignity and self-esteem. They make the distinction between" idiopathic" violent (those committed by persons who suffer from a major psychological disorder) and "normatively prescribed" violence (those committed by persons were members of a subculture of violence). Ferracuti's work might explain some youth violence against those outside the family, but does not explain violence against significant others. Glaser and Galvan [18] hypothesized that children who are isolated and from families with weak affectionate bonds are prime candidates for gang delinquency and peer- oriented deviant behavior. Another explanation of violent behavior by Bandura (1973) [19] is the social learning theory. It emphasizes the parent's last child relationship and early childhood experiences. These early experiences are thought to form the basic personality. If the training is an undesirable characteristics it will be passed on to future generations. A child who witnesses parental attempts to solve family problems through aggressive behavior is likely to incorporate such aggressive behavior. A number of researchers studied the family situation of youths involved in killing or threatening to kill their parents (Duncan and Duncan, 1971: Tanay, 1973: King, 1975: and Sorrells, 1977). [20] The studies revealed family environment characterized by turmoil, physical abuse of children, constant verbal and physical fighting between parents, and parents whose own parents had been drinkers. Tartar ET, al., 1984 [21] reported that adolescent delinquents who were sons of alcoholic fathers pictured more poorly cognitively than those whose fathers were not alcoholic. They also found that the sons of alcoholics were also more likely to have been physically abused. Lewis, et. al., (1979) [22] compared violent delinquents to a sample of less aggressive male juveniles. They found the most striking factors distinguishing the violent from the less violent were related to physical abuse. McCord (1979) [23] found that the parents that exercised significantly less supervision of males became convicted of violent crimes. Loeber et. al., found that when parents tolerated violence in the homes this acceptance of violence was generalize outside the home. [24]

In another view: Kohut 1971, 1980 found that the delinquent has a disorder of his or her sense of self arising during the separation- individuation (especially the so-called reapproachment phase) of development when their parents responded to them inadequately. The result may be either a draining and persistent regressive need to seek a kind of accepting, affirming mirror of the child's sense of omnipotence, grandiosity or a tendency to over idealize another person and merge with the person. Such persons have little tolerance either for the less than ideal nature of others or for their own deficits. They were easily overwhelmed and often chronically enraged. This rage may be projected and of course a projected identification. Kornberg (1975) [26] views the person as having a grandiose self, again arising during the separation- individuation but as a defense against early splitting of rage and envy directed toward object representation. This may persist as a constant tendency toward splitting, seen often as rapid shifts between over idealization and devaluation of the object.

One of the most difficult issues in understanding the roots of delinquent violence is that so much of the phenomena of their condition is hard for the average person to accept. [27] The callous, unthinking cruelty and gross disrespect for the victim's life can typify these youth. They appear to have no sense of preciousness of self and are seemingly indifferent to all significant human warmth and caring. Moreover, if the youth is apprehended he is arrogant rather than repentant; he's angry, haughty and demanding instead of apologetic and guilt stricken. This is truly bewildering. There has been some investigation into the nature of this narcissistic reality. The sense of self can be thought of as creating a presence in space a territory of self. It is a strange sort of space. It is the narcissistic puffing out of self. [28] The particular space thus occupied becomes very significant. That significance attaches both to his content and to his boundaries but especially to boundaries. This boundary can contain other people and often it does. The very concept of self-[29] speaks for such a state of affairs, and for the more successful narcissist it is of considerable importance to bring others within his orbit. [30] To the extent that the space of the psychological self falls somewhat close to the narcissistic realities and if one sense of what one is like and looks like is close to what the world sees, then the narcissistic state is a good balance with the real world. But, where there are radical differences, the individual faces many hazards. In the more complex cases such tyrannical tendencies lead them to become gang leaders. Then they act to protect (sometimes terrify) their own group while invading and attacking other groups.

Diggs (1950), Monahan (1957), and Cavon (1959), among others correlated statistics and arrived at the conclusion that the delinquency among Blacks is the result of the disintegration and disorganization of the black lower-class family. [31] Gangs are thus the youths early construct of a network of relationships with which black youth learn the intricacies of survival techniques and the nuances of that lifestyle that he most knows if he is to function safely and efficiently in the ghetto. The physical violent groundwork established by the aggressive family and the relationships skills learned in the ghetto have little survival value in the conventional world of **work**. In fact, the skills which may make a young man an "Executive " on the street, i.e. hustling, rapping, signifying, psyching people out, fighting and gang leadership, may also serve to make him a failure as a laborer in society.

Unfortunately, the overly aggressive behavior, violence and anger that some of our young men exhibit is learned in the home. Some angry, hostile, domineering parents rear their children by being verbally and physically abusive. They do not balance their discipline with instruction. They are always critical, judgmental, demeaning toward their sons. Their son learns how to be demeaning and hostile to others. It is because young boys learn their rage and aggressiveness from their parents that the bible warns, "Fathers, do not provoke your children to anger, but bring them up in the discipline and instruction of the Lord." (Ephesians 6:4)

PSYCHOLOGICAL FACTORS AND IMPLEMENTATION OF CHURCH MINISTRY

The information in this chapter will enlighten and educate the laity in the psychological development of adolescent African American males. The laity will be instructed on the identity crises and low self-esteem of the church's' youth. They will be taught about the enormous emotional impact of young boys being raised without a father and the psychological dynamics of gang violence. Also this data will be used to create training session for Christian Male mentoring. The laity will discover how to understand the immoral, irreverent behavior of adolescents and counsel them. The laity will learn how to bolster the self-esteem of the youth. Finally they will ascertain how to be good mentors and role models for them. They will attempt to fulfill the paternal deprivation and bond with the boys. The implementation of this ministry upon adolescent African American males will address low self-esteem, paternal deprivation and negative socialization process.

Therefore a mentoring program called, "My Brothers' Keeper", will be a part of this church ministry. Mentoring program can provide the emotional and psychological support the youth need. It may help to fulfill the father hunger these boys feel. A Mentor can provide a bridge between boyhood and manhood. Young men will learn what it is to be a responsible and respectable man. Finally there will be Liberation Lessons that will instruct adolescent African American males in their great history and potential. They'll be enlightened about the vast contributions and achievements of African Americans. It will be instilled in them that they can make significant impact on society. Despite institutional racism and social oppression they can rise to excellence like their fore parents. This will build up their self-esteem and enable them to strive to new academic heights and self- awareness. They will know that there are no limitations to what they can achieve in life. Furthermore, the young boys will be taught about their divine identity in Jesus Christ. They will learn that they are first and foremost children of God and will no longer refer to themselves or others in derogatory terms. They will no longer measure their self-worth by their money or material acquisitions. Nor will they disrespect themselves by wearing sagging pants. They will lift up their pants as well as their self-esteem and give God glory.

Chapter Two – End Notes

1   Shellie Sampson, Orientation of Black Youth (Madison: Drew University Press, 1977), p.30.

2   Jean Piaget, The Cognitive Structure and Experience in Children and Adolescents, David Children Adolescents Interpretive Essays, Jean Piaget, New York: Oxford University Press, 1974, p.6.

3   Herbert A, Otto and Sarah T.Otto, A New Perspective of Adolescent Psychological in the Schools, 1967, p. 76.

4   Kenneth B. Clark and Mamie "The Development of the Self and the Emergence of Racial Identification in Negro Pre-School Children, The Journal of Social Psychology Bulletin 1139, 10, pp.591-599.

5   Alan Ziajka, The Black Youth's Self Concept Developmental Psychology, Hindle, Dryden Press, 1972, pp.252-254. The Social Mirror of Black Youths' Self-Concept. The Looking Glass for Black Youth in American Society.

6   Sampson, p.32

7   Ibid. p.33.

8   John Bradshaw, Healing the Shame That Binds You, Communications, Deerfield, FL, p.76, 1988.

9   Kenneth Clark, Dark Ghetto, p.70. Doris B. Mosby, Toward a New Specialty of Black Psychology, Reginald Jones, Ed., p.38.

10 Nathan Hare, "Interview," The Crises, Vol. 93, no.3 March 1986:33.

11 Kenneth M. Jones, "The Black Male in Jeopardy." The Crises, Vol. 93, no.3 March 1986, pp., 27, 28

12 Ibid.

13 Hare, p. 41

14 Carol Chinelynski, "Districts off special help to young Black males," School Board News, 5 June 1990:8.

15 Samuel Osherson, Finding Our Fathers, Collier Macmillan Publishers, New York, 1986, p.9

16 Federal Bureau of Investigation (1982). Crime in the United States, 1981. Washington D.C.: U.S. Government Printing Office.

17 J. Wolfgang and Ferracuti, The Subculture of Violence. New York: Barnes and Noble, 1967.

18 P. Glassar and C.Galvin, A Framework for Family Analysis Relevant to Child Abuse, Neglect and Juvenile Delinquency. In Exploring the Relationship between Child Abuse and Delinquency, Hunner, R.J. and Walker, Y.E. Montclair, NJ: Allanheld, Osmun & Co., 1981.

19   Bandura, A. A Social Learning Analysis. Englewood Cliffs, NJ: Prentice-Hall, 1973.

20   J. Duncan and G. Duncan "Murder in the Family: A Study of some Homicidal Adolescents," American Journal of Psychiatry, 127 pp. 1498 -1502, 1971.

21   Ralph E. Tarter, et al.," Neuropsychological, Personality, and Familial Characteristics of Physically Abused Delinquents," Journal of the American Academy of Child Psychiatry, 23, 6:668 – 674.

22   D.O. Lewis, S.S. Shank, and D.A. Balla," Perinatal Difficulties, Head and Face Trauma and Child Abuse and Medical Histories of Seriously Delinquent Children," American Journal of Psychiatry pp. 419 423.

23   McCord 1979.

24   Loeber et al. 1983.

25   H. Kohut, The Analysis of the Self. New York: International Universities Press, 1971. H. Kohort, Self-Psychology: Reflections on the Present and Future. Paper read at Boston Psychoanalytical Association Symposium on Reflections on Self Psychology, Boston, and November 2, 1980.

26   O. Kernberg, Borderline Conditions and Pathological Narcissism. New York: Aronson, 1975.

27   Joseph D. Noshpitz, "Narcissism and Aggression." American Journal of Psychotherapy, Vol. XXXVIII, no. 1, Jan. 1984.

28   Ibid.

29   Kohut.

30   K. Abraham," Particular Form of Neurotic Resistance against the Psychoanalytic Method," in Selected Paper on Psychoanalysis, Hogart Press, London, 1949.
     Jones, E., "The God Complies." In Essays in Applied Psychoanalysis, International Universities Press, New York 1964.

31   Mary H.Diggs," Some Problems and Needs of Negro Children Revealed by Comparative Delinquency and Crime Statistics," Journal of Negro Education, vol. 19 pp.290- 297, 1950.
     T. P. Monahan," Family Status and the Delinquent Child Reappraisal and Some New Findings," Social Forces, pp. 250 -258, 1957.Ruth Shonie Caven, Negro Family Disorganization and Juvenile Delinquency," Journal of Negro Education, Vol. 28, pp. 44-46, 1959.

Chapter Three

Spiritual Chains of Young African American Males

"He who is conceived in a cage yearns for the cage."
Yevgeny Yevtushenko

"Do you know that to whom you present yourselves
slaves to obey, you are that ones' slaves to whom you
obey, whether of sin leading to death, or of obedience
leading to righteousness?" Romans 6:16

The spiritual chains that foster drug dependency and drug dealing amongst adolescent African American males are important to understanding the nature of their spiritual slavery. The links in their spiritual chain are dysfunctional families, television, Rap music, violent video games and codependent churches. All of these teach immoral, unethical, violent behavior and unwittingly create the spiritual chain for youth oppression. These young men had been chained at an early age by their dysfunctional families. Also their families were ineffective in teaching or exemplifying Christian values which hampered their spiritual growth. The church either ignored or rejected the youth cultural experiences and were unable to translate the gospel in an idiom they could appreciate. Furthermore the church's inability to render relevant moral and religious instruction created a spiritual void in the youth. This existential emptiness is fulfilled by boob- tube values and irreverent rappers who promote sexual promiscuity, conspicuous consumerism, violent behavior, misogyny, substance abuse and nihilism. Dysfunctional families, poor teaching, ineffective church ministries , corrupt media, create high risk black males which end up enslaved to drugs and confined to corruption.

YOUNG BLACK MALES EXISTENTIAL VACUUM

Through surveys, essays and interviews with adolescent African American males within the church, ex-drug dealers, drug users and high risk adolescent African American males, we discovered their anti-religious, existential vacuum. Many of them were deist or Christian nominalist. As deist, they believed in a Supreme Being or God but they didn't believe in following a particular religion or moral ethical code of conduct. They believed God of grace and not judgment. As one young man said," I do believe in God, without the man upstairs I wouldn't be here." He and others limit or define a personal God who does not make them accountable for their immoral behavior. Others were Christian nominalist and were raised by religious mothers who took them to church as children and rarely attended as adolescents. They believed that Jesus Christ was their Savior but did not respect Him as the Lord of their life. They practiced what Dietrich Bonhoeffer called" cheap grace". They essentially believed in having grace without paying the cost of discipleship. [1] They had faith but not works. They wanted the crown of life without bearing the cross. Many of them saw the gross discrepancy between the immoral way Christians lived and the precepts of the gospel. The boys saw how their parent(s) rarely read the Bible and attended church. They were spiritual but not religious. Most of the youth came from families that did not emphasize Sunday school. They went to Sunday school when they were children but refused to go when they became teenagers. None of the youth were encouraged to read their Bibles or pray. In fact they said their parents or guardians rarely read the Bible. Also according to the survey their parents were Christian nominalist who practiced "cheap grace." Consequently, they went to church and periodically encouraged their boys to come to church. Christianity was rarely stressed in the home. Some of young boys said their mothers "preached" to them about the dangers of drugs but they had liquor bottles hidden away. Some admitted that their parents didn't practice what they preach. They saw them cursing, smoking drinking, fighting, gambling and they questioned the credibility of their parents faith. Many of the boys who had a father in the home never saw their fathers go to church, pray, or read the Bible.

The lack of religious foundation made it difficult for the boys to make good moral choices. Their spiritual vacuum predisposes them to immoral and addictive behavior. It is no wonder young people were becoming drug dealers and users when there is no Christian teaching and practice within the home. It is not a coincidence that the most influential person in the life of adolescent African American male is a Rapper. Most of the young black males admired and revered Rappers and their music. Some of these teens idolize the Rappers and tried to imitate them in dress, mannerism and conduct. The most disturbing fact, is that the young black males could recite many of the lyrics of rap music but could not recite one single scripture. They knew who Little Wayne was but could not tell you who Moses was. They could tell you every hit song Drake had but could not recite the Lord's Prayer. Young African American males received their moral-ethical beliefs from rappers and not their pastors or Sunday School Teachers. Our young Black Males had an existential vacuum that was filled by the corrupt value system espoused by low life rappers.

RELIGIOUS DEVELOPMENT OF BLACK MALES

Our religious maturity is based on our childhood experiences and psychological development. Religious development stems from our psychosocial growth. 1 Gerkins, "Living Document", points out that our primary images of God and sense of selfhood are developed from an infant's relationship with his mother. The construction of a true- self is created by a mother who generally responds to needs. If the mother insists that the infant conform to her narcissistic need, the child develops a false self which has a "narcissistic construction of the world." [2]

The enormous social and financial pressures impinged upon some single African American mother may lead her to unconsciously raise her sons with a narcissistic construction of the world. The self-centeredness and hedonistic character of some adolescent African American males may stem from their neonatal experiences. The overwhelming responsibility of raising African American males is generally left to single impoverished African American women. Young black males learn to negotiate around women with authority. They don't learn how to handle men in authority. Heavy exposure to a positive adult male role model is essential to the healthy moral development of a male child and being nurtured by a domineering mother may lead to deviant behavior. Moreover the sense of being emasculated and internal stress of the situation may lead to overly aggressive and violent behavior. Moreover adolescence is a period of intense physiological and psychological flux in which the adolescent struggles to stabilize his identity. [3] Religious identity is important at this time as they wrestle with their sense of guilt and shame. [4] The religious or spiritual identity of some young African American males is due to a lack of a positive male role model, a domineering mother and social oppression.

The adolescent faith is shaped in the crucible of all of their inner struggles and in their psycho-social development. It is their faith that undergirds their operative theology. It is their faith that determines what is most important to them and how they behave .Fowler's book, "The Stages of Faith", explicates what faith really means. It is not a belief, creed or religious colloquialism. Faith is the way we make and maintain meaning in life. It is a human universal phenomenon which speaks to self- identity and ultimate concern in life. One need not to be religious to have faith." Faith is deeper, richer, or more personal. It is an orientation of the personality to oneself, to one's neighbors, to the universe; a total response; a way of seeing whatever one sees and of handling whatever one handles... Faith, therefore, involves vision. It is made of knowing, of acknowledgment. One commits oneself to that which is known or acknowledged, and lives legally, with life and character being shaped by that commitment. The Hebrew (uman) the Greek (pistup) and the Latin (credo) words for faith parallel those from Hindu sources. They cannot mean belief or believing... faith involves an alignment of the will, resting of the heart in one's ultimate concern. [5]

DRUG DEALERS HENOTHEISTIC FAITH

Since faith is ones' ultimate concern, it is easy to discern what kind of faith that self-centered, hedonistic drug dealers demonstrated. It is not a polytheistic faith that has many interests and values. [6] Nor is it a brief transient faith of intense commitments. [7] It is not a radical monotheism in which they are solely bound to a particular the community that places its identification with a universal community. The faith of the adolescent African American male drug dealer is more henotheistic faith in that they engage in sui projects or projects of and projects a self-justification. Causa Sui henotheism finally ends up in our worshiping at an altar on which sets the faintly smiling image of our own ego. [9] Its content is centered on power and with extensions and guarantors of the self as center. Success, power, prestige, wealth and fame and the like are not end in themselves. They serve, rather, as guarantors of the worth and significance of the self." [10] The drug dealers that were interviewed had enormous egos which manifested in their need to control the lives of addicts and wield influence in the community. For many of them there projects of self- vindication included buying expensive cars, gaining more drug territory ,conspicuous consumerism, pimping women ,gross demonstrations of their power, and killing rival gangs. One drug dealer bragged, "There is nothing I can't get. If I wanted cars, women, money, homes, clothes, jewelry anything I want is mine. There isn't anyone out there who can stop me I'm a bad. Look at this Rolex watch. Look at my gold chains and my fresh Air Jordan's. I'm a bad man." In spite of his bravado, he was really hiding his deep sense of shame and feeling of worthlessness. All of his machismo and materialism is a manifestation of his henotheistic faith. Faith that is centered on himself and his own worldly accomplishments. His pride and arrogance makes him think he is better than anyone else. But the bible reminds us, "If anyone wants to be proud, he should be proud of what the Lord has done. It is not what a man thinks and says of himself that is important. It is what God thinks of him." II. Corinthians 10:17-18

DYSFUNCTIONAL BLACK FAMILIES

The lack of morality and spirituality in African American males is partly due to dysfunctional Black families. The black family is in crisis as it exhibits dysfunctional, destructive, dehumanizing behavior that ultimately leads to shame-based nature of some adolescent African American males which fosters teenage school dropout, juvenile delinquency, violence and drug abuse. Dysfunctional families are characterized by denial and delusional thinking. Boundaries can be rigid, flexible, controlled and the individual exists for the family. [11] In the marriage, the partners feel shame and inadequacy. Each chooses to pursue their own needs as a way to get complete. Once married, each focuses on getting rather than giving. Conflict, power and great anxiety result. Children enter a family with dependent needs. Since parents are needy they can't fulfill children's needs. The parent's abuse the children to get their own needs met. This is abusive behavior. The youths carry their past family systems with them. This includes the discipline and child-rearing techniques with which they grew up. Parents with low self-esteem have no way to teach their children self-esteem. As new parents they carry the same diseased role model to their children. Parents can't teach values and social concern if they don't have it themselves. Dysfunctional families are multi-generational. [13]

THE SINS OF THE FATHERS

In the Old Testament, the biblical writers refer to dysfunctional multi-generational families as sinful. The "sins of the Fathers" are passed down from one generation to another. In the Black community's context, the sins of absentee fathers, overly aggressive behavior, addictive personality, self-hatred and toxic shame are learned by children who teach it to their children. We wonder why young boys act the way they do, but if we looked at some of their parents we would understand. Some of these boys are being raised in dysfunctional families that have inadvertently taught them to be evil. The parents must share the brunt of the moral responsibility for raising social deviants. The parents must repent of their sins for not raising their child with biblical principles.

In interviews with the boys of the church, most felt neglected by their parents. Many of them said their parents were too busy to spend time with them. The boys felt ignored and rejected by their parents. Several youth expressed dismay over the harsh discipline they received from their parent or parents. They felt belittled. When they did something wrong they were not only severely punished but also ridiculed. The autocrat parental style stifled individual moral development. In a church survey, it was discovered that there are many dysfunctional families. Dysfunctional families operate with the following results:

1. Problems are denied, therefore, never solved.
2. Desires, perceptions, and thoughts are rigidly controlled.
3. Communication is indirect, incongruent, and vague.
4. Anyone trying to get is needs met is called selfish.
5. Family members must conform to family rules; they cannot be different.
6. Anxiety level is high.
7. Parents are undisciplined disciplinarian.
8. Roles are rigid and assigned.
9. Atmosphere is grim. [14]

In church surveys, with young African American males we discovered that their homes manifested the above characteristics. Many of the boys rarely talked with their fathers and their fathers rarely discussed things with them. The boys always felt that they were receiving orders, correction or instructions about something. In some of the single-parent homes, the mothers were perceived as being extremely authoritative, setting law and abusively enforcing it. Almost all of the boys didn't think that their parents ever listened to their concerns or feelings.

Most of the families, where the boys were raised, showed all the signs compulsivity. Compulsivity is the core addiction which is defined by the World Health Organization as a pathological relationship to a mood altering event, person, experience or thing that produces harmful consequences in one's life. There are all kinds of mood altering addictions. One could be addicted to, material objects, drugs and food. Or one could be addicted to activities like sleep, entertainment, sports or gambling .Some people are addicted to their parents or destructive relationships. There are those who are addicted to emotions like rage-aholics, sad-aholics, and joy-aholics. These addictions are result of the mismanagement of emotions. It is a diseased lifestyle that is rooted in family and affects everyone.

The most common addiction in America is the addiction to people. In every type of family plagued by, sexual addiction, sexual abuse, eating disorders, physical abuse, emotional and moral abuse all the members of the family are diseased. This form of disease has come to be called codependency or people addiction.

THE CAPTIVITY OF CODEPENDENCY

Melodies Beattie outstanding book," Codependency no more" shares that codependency is an unhealthy relationship to a mood altering person that has damaging consequences. Codependents give up their own needs and wants. Like all addiction, codependency has at its core a shame-based person. [15] Such people feel worthless and believe they do not have a right to depend on another person to get their needs met. Instead they react to or live according to another person's feelings needs and wants. The codependent is really a slave to others. They live their whole life dependent on others. They are held captive by the feelings, behavior, addictions and lifestyle of others. Codependency can occur on a one-to-one basis or with a group of people to which one pledges gives up their own identity. Codependence manifest the following characteristics:

1. Difficulty in identifying and expressing feelings and desires.
2. Difficulty in forming or maintaining close relationships.
3. Perfectionism-unrealistic of self and others. The drive for perfection is always rooted in damaged integrity.
4. Rigid or stuck attitudes and behavior.
5. Difficulty in making changes.
6. Feeling overly responsible for other people.
7. Difficulty in making decisions.

8. Enmeshed boundaries—they don't know their individual limits within the co-dependents relationship.
9. General feelings of being flawed and power less over one's life. [16]

Some of the adolescent African American males were raised in dysfunctional families where their mothers were codependents. They grew up in families where there was unclear communication. Some mothers found it extremely difficult to effectively talk to their sons about their drug activity. Moreover the boys rarely shared their true feelings with their mothers and never with their absent fathers. They repressed their feelings and pretended to conform to the house rules. A lot of the mothers were in denial about the substance abuse of their teenage sons. They did not want to believe that their boys could do anything wrong.

SPIRITUAL SLAVERY

The substance abuse of adolescent African American males and the codependency experienced by their mothers is a form of spiritual slavery. Spiritual slavery manifest itself in teenagers compulsively abusing street drugs and their parent futility trying to control them. Taking drugs and being unable to refrain from them is a form of slavery. Unfortunately, many young African American males are slaves to heroin, marijuana, cocaine and other narcotics. They will lie, cheat, steal and even kill to abuse drugs. So great is their bondage to do drugs that one young African American male drug addict attacked Rosa Parks, the Mother of the Civil Rights Movement, in her Detroit home! This dastardly deed was done by a drug addicted, spiritual slave. Ironically, Rosa Parks had fought all of her life to set Black people free but her attacker and others were still in bondage to their sins. Spiritual slavery to drugs has the potential to eradicate all the gains of the civil rights movement and devastate our entire community. One drug dealer selling drugs in our community can do more danger than one-hundred Klu Klux Klan members.

The drug dealer is not only a slave master of the drug addict but he also is a slave. The drug dealer may act like he is in charge but he is really a slave to prosperity and privilege. He is a spiritual slave to sin and drug dealing.

So great is his captivity, that he would sell drugs to his own relatives and destroy their lives. Personally, I knew a drug dealer who was aware of the fact that his own sister was strung out on crack cocaine but did nothing to stop her from doing drugs. Moreover he sold her drugs! Tragically, she died in a drug den where his drugs were sold and used. This drug dealer is a spiritual slave that needs to be set free from his drug dealing. He needs the gospel of Jesus Christ preached to him to save his soul and set him free. I preached the gospel to this drug dealer but he refused the gospel and his freedom. The bible is right, "The wages of sin is death, but the gift of God is eternal life in Jesus Christ." Romans 6:23

What is equally disturbing is that drug dealers and substance abusers can live in a home and no one says or does anything about it. The denial in the family is so strong that no one in wants to admit to drug use. In some cases, the family members actually profit from the drug dealers enterprise. Some family members receive monetary gifts that are used to buy their silence and complicity. The family member of the drug dealer will be given money, cars, homes and even legitimate businesses to sanction and support the drug dealer. The co-dependent family of the drug dealers are just as guilty as the drug dealer for the drug related crimes in the community. The family members of drug dealers are co-dependent and spiritual slaves because they either profit from the drug dealer or attempt to control his behavior. It is a sin for parents not to confront their drug dealing or addicted teen about his substance abuse. Parents must love their children enough to tell them about Jesus Christ, get their kids in therapy, call the police or kick them out of the house. They must show these drug dealers the "tough love" they need to be set free from their spiritual slavery. They must love their boys enough to tell them the truth. They must not lie to the police. The parent must be willing to tell the truth about their criminal son who is creating chaos in the community. The bible says, "Do not tell a lie about someone else. Do not join with the sinful to say something that will hurt someone." Exodus 23:1

MEDIA INFLUENCE ON YOUNG AFRICAN AMERICAN MALES

The media influences the spirituality of adolescent African American males. Television, videogames and rap music instill immoral values, unethical, and ungodly behavior. The media mesmerizes our boy's with salacious, vicious, irreligious images which corrupts their minds, harden their hearts and enslave their souls. Furthermore it brainwashes them with sexual immorality, conspicuous consumerism, and glorifies violence. Consequently many of our youth become vulnerable to the ungodly values and wicked ways of the world. The media constantly tempts and lures them to sin. Eventually the youth yield to temptation and are driven to fulfill the lust of the flesh. They become slaves to sin and the media continues to indoctrinate them to be subservient to their sins. The media is responsible for warping America's moral foundation and enslaving millions. The bible warns us, "For everything that is in the world does not come from the Father. The desires of our flesh and the things our eyes see and want and the pride of this life come from the world. The world and all its desires will pass away. But the man who obeys God and does what He wants done will live forever." I. John 2:16-17

TELEVISION AND THE MEDIA

Surveys have shown that children and youth watch television more than any other activity. The average American child spends more time watching TV before entering first grade than the child spent in school through the first six grades. Many adolescents spent four years a day watching television. A current Nielsen television index determined that children ages 2 to 5 watch TV 22 hours and 29 minutes per week. Those children ages 6 to 11 watch 19 hours and 30 minutes per week. It has been estimated that the average male watches three thousand entire days of television by 65th year. [17]

The television practices of African American households are 23 hours a week more than in other households. Investigators found black children age 17 and under were found to watch T.V one hour and six minutes more than nonblack children. There are detrimental effects of African American children watching television for a long period of time. Malloy a Washington Post columnist points out that black youth receive immoral values that encourage them to commit murders identical to those on television shows.[18] The column goes on to say that in his opinion children of this generation have an attitude of greed and selfishness. Television promotes mindless materialism, glamorizes violence, and instant gratification. [19]

Dr. Postman wrote about televisions detrimental effects. According to him television communicates projects images and perceptions that are unrealistic and immoral. Most children and youth are unable to shift between fact and fantasy. Therefore television should be closely monitored because:

- The inability of a person to accumulate knowledge-based experiences;
- The limits of interaction at home and in the community.
- The creation of an impression among youth that all problems can be solved easily: and,
- TV robs youngsters of their childhood. [20]

In interviews with adolescent African American males it was ascertained that the many of them watch and play a lot of video games. One of the more popular video games is called" Grand Theft Auto." In this videogame the youth is allowed to imagine himself as a drug dealer going about stealing cars, selling drugs, engaging in sexually promiscuous acts, beating up elderly people and even killing police officers. Children and youth spend hours playing this game that desensitizes them to acts of violence and criminality. This and other violent video games impact the young person's moral consciousness. He may never do these acts but he is definitely been desensitize to them.

SPIRITUALITY OF RAP MUSIC

Another prominent influence on adolescent African American males is the Rap musician and their music. Rap music first emerged in the late 70s by Kurtis Blow. It is a mixture of rhymes and memorable phrases with a catchy rhythm. It has become the most prominent music among African American youth. It can be heard blaring out of car windows, in school hallways or from street corners. Rap music is listened to constantly, memorized, internalized and acted out in everyday life. It is the dominant sound and passion of African American youth. It represents some of their cultural expressions, values, yearnings, frustrations, anger, morals, and political social perspectives. What the Psalms were to the tribes of Israel so is Rap music to many youth. It is music therapy that makes them feel good and gets them through the day. Whatever they are feeling and thinking can be found in rap music. There is a spirituality to rap music. Rap music is spiritual because it speaks to the passions, feelings and fantasies of many young people. There is some rare positive rap music but most share these common negative values or beliefs:

1. HEDONISTIC – Rap music emphasizes pleasure seeking. It promotes sexual promiscuity. Many rap songs talk about having sex with various woman.

2. MISOGYNISTIC – Rap music demeans women as sexual objects. Women are depicted as strippers, prostitutes and sexual creatures.

3. MATERIALISTIC – Rap music promulgates mindless materialism and conspicuous consumerism. Often the rappers promote themselves by driving expensive exotic cars, wearing gaudy jewelry and million dollar mansions.

4. NIHILISTIC – Rap music has an anti-authoritarian edge to it. It promotes lawlessness and rebelliousness

5. CANABALISTIC – Rap music is cannibalistic in that it spews hatred and hostility against others. The racial hatred can be heard in the use of the "n" word that was used when Blacks were hung, beaten, enslaved, castrated and exploited. For rappers to refer to each other and themselves with the "n" word is a form of self-hatred or cannibalism. It degrades an entire race of people. There is a lot of hostility and violence in rap music. Often rappers talk about killing and shooting people. It is cannibalistic to try to destroy one another.

6. NARCISSITIC – Rappers tend to glorify and magnify themselves. Their self-centeredness can be heard throughout their songs. Their self- absorption and self-promotion is endless.

Some of the more popular rappers amongst young males are Little Wayne, Drake, Chief Keef, Big Shaun, Meek Mill and Eminem. These rappers and others are admired and revered to the point of idolization. Many young males listen to every word that these men espouse. They spend hours listening and repeating their licentious lyrics. What young people refuse to get or could not get from the church they receive from rappers. Rappers are teaching, preaching and singing an ungodly gospel that is perverting the minds and corrupting the character of our young people. Rappers and their music have a profound impact on the heart, mind and soul of young African American males. It is through Rap music that youth internalize a corrupt culture, vacuous values and unscrupulous norms of behavior. Most popular Rappers are emulated because of their mesmerizing music, successful image, and nihilistic message which speaks to the heart of adolescence. Moreover young African American males listen and adhere to rappers immoral values rather than those promoted by the church, family and school. The results are malignant, angry, hostile, debased behavior and spiritual oppression.

Our Lord and Savior Jesus Christ once said, "By your words you will be acquitted and by your words you will be condemned." He was pointing out that the words that we carelessly use are weighed, measured and judged by God. We will be held accountable for every profane word, every curse, racial slur, demeaning message, salacious song and nasty Rap song that we utter. Rappers who espouse these negative words must understand that not only are the children and youth listening, GOD IS LISTENING!! God listens and is concerned about the filthy words that some of these Rappers are espousing. Their licentious lyrics reveal a dirty soul that desperately in need of the blood of Jesus Christ to save and sanctify it. All of these Rappers who rap conspicuous consumerism, sexual promiscuity, glorify violence, use derogatory words must repent of their sins. Some of them need to know Jesus Christ as their personal Lord and Savior. All of them should use the musical gift that God has given them in a positive, uplifting way and to glorify Him. I pray for the day when Little Wayne, Eminem, Jay Z and others will stop using profanity and glorify the name of Jesus Christ. I pray for the day when these Rappers will clean up their lyrics and begin to rap about the gospel of Jesus Christ. Can you imagine the millions of young souls they could save? Some may think that I am dreaming. But what they do not realize is, that if God can convert my sinful soul, He can change anybody. If God can deliver me from my sinful, worldly ways and put me in His pulpit, He can do it with anybody. There is no Rapper, Gangster, drug dealer, drug addict or criminal that God cannot forgive, redeem, save, transform, consecrate, sanctify to His glory. So those of us who believe in the power of prayer, must keep praying for the salvation of these Rappers. We must never give up on them because "with God all things are possible."

CO-DEPENDENT CHURCH

"I was a stranger and you did not invite me in, I needed clothes and you did not clothe me, I was sick and in prison and you did not look after me." Matthew 25:43

The other link in the spiritual chain of adolescent African American youth comes from the church. One day I saw an unconscious, inebriated young man on the church steps, and Sunday worshippers stepping over him to get into the church. I asked someone, "Who is more sick, the addict or the person who ignores or rejects him?" I firmly believe that the self-righteous Christian who vilifies, judges and ignores addicts is spiritually sick. Moreover the church that does not directly engage in ministry that liberates addicts, is pathological and codependent. Therefore the church is a co-conspirator of the spiritual slavery of young African American males. Its operative theology adds and abets the spiritual oppression of young Black males.

The church can be a codependent institution in that it can inadvertently maintain the proliferation and profiteering of drugs and alcohol. Some churches are guilty of fostering substance abuse because of their lack of relevant youth programs, spiritual elitism, esoteric preaching, social complacency, Eurocentric theology, social snobbery, sexism and confusion over outreach ministries. The transgressions of the codependent Church can create a spiritual void, exacerbate the fragmentation of the family, give sanction to social stratification and deepen an inferiority complex which can lead to drug and alcoholic addiction. The codependent congregation has a false consciousness in relation to themselves and chemically addicted neighbors. Some church people feel morally superior to addicts and judge, condemned and ostracize them. Ironically they are incapable of perceiving and accepting their own sinful shortcomings. Their pride and prejudice blinds them from their own transgressions and bad attitude. Consequently the codependent congregation honestly believe that they are morally superior to drug dealers and crack users. Their social and spiritual snobbery is unwarranted and untenable. The Bible teaches "all have sinned and fallen short of the glory of God" and there is none righteous. Therefore the codependent church is practicing a fallacious falsehood and hypocritically denounces addicts and ignores its own sins and shortcomings. The bible speaks to this kind of church when it states, "There are people who are pure in their own eyes, but are not washed from their own dirt. There is a kind, O, how proud are his eyes." Proverbs 30:12-13

YOUNG DRUG ADDICTS DISRUPT WORSHIP SERVICE

The church that I pastored had operative theology of codependence. We were in effect enabling young alcoholics and drug users. Also the church obliquely benefited from this immoral interdependence with the drug community. The following actual event typifies our codependency. We were having an evening worship service, when two rowdy young black males came into the sanctuary and sat in the back of the church. One of them wore a red head band, blue jeans and gym shoes. The other wore a red shirt with a college insignia on it and sneakers. None of the worshipers notice them until they began to make a lot of noise laughing and joking. Then most of the members were looking back at them periodically. As we took up the offering they appeared to get really quiet and whispered among themselves. I thought that they were casing the place to steal the offering. At the close of the service they began to get loud again. One of them shouted something at me. Some of the members got nervous, clutched their purses, and began to leave. I invited the young man and his friend to come to the front of the church and join a prayer circle. As they walked down the aisle, I discerned that they were drunk or high. One of them was drunk. He had red eyes and his speech was slurred. The smell of liquor rose from his breath and he stumbled as he walked. The other one appeared to be high on something. His eyes were dilated and he had an angry look on his face. His fist were clenched and his body seemed poised to pounce on someone. His voice and verbiage was harsh and violent. I looked at the expressions and postures of the congregants. One of our male members left and got a stick and stood outside of the sanctuary. Another man went and stood behind the man looking on with disgust. One woman said." You need to be born again and know the Lord."

The young man boldly declared," I don't need the Lord. You need him, in fact I am the Lord. I am God Almighty!" He walked up to me as if to pick a fight. He was a foot from my face and shouted," I came to check up on you and see if you know what you're doing." I tried to respond as graciously as I could." You're right. We are all sinners and need God's forgiveness. I'm glad you did come and check up on me because I need your prayers. Would you pray with us?" I asked everyone to hold hands as I prayed passionately pleading for God's grace to permeate the sanctuary and our hearts. At the end of the prayer the drunken young man passed out and fell in the middle of the prayer circle. After we woke him he began embracing everyone. Many of the women recoiled from his exuberant advances. The men watched with caution and concern standing beside the young boys. One of the ladies whispered," They are just disgusting. Why did they have to come here?" A couple of us embraced both of the young man and escorted them to the door.

Later I talked to the members about this challenging encounter. Some of them were thankful and relieved that nothing really bad happened. They were happy that no one was harmed and the boys didn't steal the money. Many conceded that they were really apprehensive and were unable to pray. A multitude of them were indignant that they were drunk. Even a couple of recovering adult alcoholics acted with disgust and denounced their unrighteous behavior. Alarmingly none of the congregants comment spotlighted the exigencies of the young boys and their future. No one asked what will happen to the youths. No one inquired how the church could be of assistance to young people with substance abuse problems. We didn't even consider that the boys might have been sincere worshipers and became agitated with our prejudice and apprehension. They did not try to steal the offering. It might have all been in our imagination and our ungrounded fear of young black men. It dawned on me that we had failed miserably in reaching out to them. We might have been entertaining Angels unaware. We're more concerned with our noses and nickels than the spiritual welfare of these boys. The boys were not the only ones who were high at the worship service. We were high on our pride and arrogance and self-righteousness. The boy's sin was their drunkenness, our sin was our prejudice. The boy's sickness was drugs or sickness was our complacency. Helen Keller is right, "We have found a cure for many things except the apathy of human beings."

THE CHURCHES SPIRITUAL SICKNESS

The drug addict and the alcoholic were not the only ones who were sick, the church members were sick in our complacency and hypocrisy. We were the ones who were really sick. We had a spiritual sickness that hardened our hearts with apathy, blinded our eyes with pride and dulled our consciousness with a superficial religiosity. Dr. Martin Luther King Jr. spoke to our spiritual sickness and ruined religiosity when he wrote, "A religion true to its nature must also be concerned about man's social conditions. Religion deals with both earth and heaven both time and eternity. Religion operates not only in the vertical plane but also on the horizontal. It seeks to not only to integrate men with God but integrate men with men and each man with himself. This means at bottom that the Christian gospel is a two-way road. On the one hand it seeks to change the souls of men thereby unite them with God on the other hand it seeks to change the environmental conditions of men so that the soul will have a chance after it is changed. Any religion that professes to be concerned with the soul of men and not concerned with the slums that condemn them, economic conditions that strangle them, the social conditions that cripple them, is as dry as dust religion. Such a religion the kind that the Marxist like to see an opiate of the people." [21]

Unfortunately, many Christian churches like mine practiced a religion that anesthetizes them from the psychological, and spiritual problems that produced drug dependency among young African American males. Our churches have no idea the daily temptations and struggles of the youth deal with nor are they aware of the spiritual, psychological chains of young drug dealers and substance abusers. The church either sanctimoniously denounces them, benignly neglects them or is in consternation of them. Consequently the institutional church has created an operative theology that has made it impervious to the "endangered species". In spite of the senseless death, imprisonment, criminalization and unemployment of young black males, many churchgoers are comfortable and complacent. Hence urban communities suffer from moral disintegration and social economic destitution. Drugs and culprit conduct run amok in the community while the church anesthizes itself with a cathartic spiritualism and archaic legalism. Poverty and powerlessness immerses the neighborhood while the church espouses irrelevant essays that have no relationship to the oppressed. It is no wonder that many protestant churches are closing and drug dens opening with alarming frequency. It should be no prize that our Houses of Prayer are empty islands unto themselves while our young are drowning in chemical hallucinogens. It's understandable that many mothers are praying in their pews while their sons wallow in prison. It should not surprise us that young black males deride the pastor, ignore the gospel, reject the church, wear sagging pants and live immoral lives. The institutional church is partly responsible for the moral decline of society and the enslavement of young Black males.

The information used in this chapter will be used to develop training sessions that will liberate the laity from the characteristics of the Co-dependent Church. The laity will be liberated from their co-dependency, ageism, and ignorance of youth culture, apathy and religious self-righteousness. Furthermore they will be taught the healing and liberation mission of the church. They will be trained to become Christian Mentors to guide Black Boys into a saving knowledge of Jesus Christ, instruct them in Christian Conflict Resolution, guide them in a Rite of Passage program and indoctrinate them with Liberation Lessons.

Chapter Three – End Notes

1   Shellie Sampson, Jr., The Orientation and Identity of Black Youth, Drew University, p. 30.
2   Charles Gerkin, Living Document, Abingdon Press, Nashville, TN, 1984, p. 86.
3   Sampson, p. 33.
4   Ibid. p. 34.
5   James Fowler, The Stages of Harper & San Francisco, 1981, p.13.
6   Ibid. p. 23.
7   Ibid.
8   Ibid.
9   Ibid.
10 Ibid.
11 John Bradshaw, On the Family: A Revolutionary Way of Self-Discovery, Health Communications, Pompano Beach, FL, 1988, p. 18.
12 Ibid. p. 49.
13 Ibid.
14 p.23.
15 p. 19.
16 p. 49.
17 Jeffrey M. Johnson, The Black Male: The New Bald Eagle, Management Plus, 1989, p. 24.
18 p. 25.
19 p. 26.
20 p. 27.
21 Coretta Scott King, The Words of Martin Luther King, Newmarket Press, New York, p.36.

Chapter Four

"They are blind guides. If a blind man leads a blind man, both will fall into the pit." Matthew 15:14

Liberation of The Laity

The laity need to be liberated before they can liberate adolescent African American males. They need to be liberated from their ignorance about youth adolescent behavior, drug culture, self-centeredness, and self-righteous religiosity. The laity need to be set free from the lies that they have been told about themselves and young African American males. They need to be set free from their pride and arrogance that make them think that they have not sinned and fallen short of the glory of God. They must stop believing the racist lie that all young African American males are inherently evil, thugs, gangsters and social deviants beyond the redemption of God. We must repent of our hypocrisy that makes us judge heroin addicts in the street and ignore alcoholics in the home. We must confess our apathy and complacency. For too long we have watched our young Black males die at an early age and do nothing about it. For too long we have lived by the philosophy, "see no evil, hear no evil, and speak no evil. " We have pretended not to see our youth selling drugs. We have learned to ignore hearing the gun shots and cries for help. We have been appallingly silent as gangsters terrorize our neighborhood. It is time for the people of God to repent of our apathy and indifference. The Bible tells us, "If my people who are called by my name, will turn from their wicked ways, seek my face and humble themselves, then I will hear from heaven and heal their land."(II. Chronicles 5:7) If we want our youth to be healed, then the people of God must repent of their social apathy and moral complacency. It is time for the Church to stand up and speak up and be my brothers' keeper.

A major part of the problem is our spiritual ignorance and lack of understanding our youth. Many of us want to do something for our youth but we do not know what to do. Our hearts are right, but we lack knowledge and wisdom. Many of us don't understand the culture, struggles, perspectives, spirituality and behavior of our young people. Many laity don't fully understand the biblical and theological foundations for youth ministry. Our lack of knowledge has alienated us from our youth and inadvertently destroyed many lives. If we do not understand the liberation ministry of our Lord amongst the least, lost and left out and how it applies today, then we are co-conspirators in the oppression of our youth. All the lying, cheating, stealing, drug dealing and killing is partly due to our lack of knowledge. The bible warns us, "My people are destroyed because of a lack of knowledge." If we want to stop failing our youth, it is time for us to go back to school and pick up the good book. We need to read our bibles and study youth culture that we may be able to do effective ministry.

Therefore in this chapter we will provide biblical and theological information about the liberation and healing ministries of the church. Moreover there will be training sessions about adolescent African American males that will prepare the laity to engage in liberation ministry. The lay training sessions stem from readings from the Holy Scriptures, sociological information, psychological sources and Afro-centric liberation theology that will fully educate the laity for ministry.

The eight individual training sessions will be based on the information in the previous chapters. The laity training sessions are : the Healing church ; the Liberating church ; Black theology and Liberation; Liberating the Soul ; Liberating the Mind ; Liberating Young Black Males within an Oppressive society ; Psychological Background of Young Black Drug

Dealers ; Spiritual Background of Young Black Males ; Young Black Males and Drugs ; Liberating Ministry and Social Background of Young Black Males. Each laity training session begins with an opening prayer and scripture reading. Then there is a brief lesson, followed by discussion of scripture readings and closing prayer. Once the churches laity undergo these eight training sessions they will be equipped to do liberation ministry for young African American males.

LAITY TRAINING SESSION: THE HEALING CHURCH

OPENING PRAYER

SCRIPTURE READING: I. Corinthians 12:12-27

What is the truth about the church? First, we must distinguish between the institutional church and the "Body of Christ", the "Kingdom of God". The historical institutional church can never get away from the fact that it has always sanctioned a racist, sexist, classist status quo. Rarely has it identified and fought for the oppressed. More often than not the institutional church has sided with the rich and powerful of society. Consequently the poor and underprivileged have been neglected and rejected by society. This is especially true of society's mistreatment of young African American males. They are the least, the lost and the left out. The institutional church is guilty of ignoring the plight and the oppression of these young boys. The only thing that makes the church holy is the Lamb of God who takes away the sins of the world. It is only through Christ and with Christ that the people of God are redeemed and set free from their sins. Therefore what makes the church holy is God. As Hans Kung points out, "It is God who distinguishes the church and sets it apart, marks it out for his own and makes it holy by winning power over the hearts of men through his Holy Spirit by establishing his reign, by justifying and sanctifying the sinner and thereby founding the communion of saints. This is why we do not simply believe in the Holy Church, but believe in God who makes the church Holy. This holiness being the work of Gods' Spirit among men is not something seen, but something that is revealed to those who in faith open their hearts to the sanctifying spirit of God." [1]

The institutional church is full of sinners and has no innate virtue within it. It is fair to say that the church is a hospital for sin sick souls and provides spiritual healing for the heart, mind and soul. Therefore everyone is in need of the grace of God and His healing touch. We all need healing. The sinner and saint; the Holy Roller and the party goer; the rich and the poor; the drug addict and the co-dependent all need the grace of God. No one can judge or condemn anyone. The laity must not look down their noses at young African-American male drug dealers. They are no better than them. Laity are enslaved as well as the substance abusers. It is only by the grace of God that the laity can be saved, sanctified and set free. They need to be reminded that is only by "grace that they are saved, not through works lest any man should boast." (Ephesians 2:8, 9) The laity need to be healed of their self-righteousness and the young African American males need to be healed of their substance abuse.

GOD OUR HEALER

The bible refers to God as Jehovah Rephkah our healer. (Exodus 26:2) Isaiah the prophet said of Christ "He was wounded for our transgressions .He was bruised for our iniquities and by His stripes we are healed." All throughout the New Testament it records Jesus Christ healing the sick, making the mute talk and the lame walk. Jesus healed the people of all kinds of infirmities. The same God who set the captives free back then, is the same God who can set the captives free today. There is no sickness that God can't heal. No bondage that God can't break. No demon that God can't defeat. No sorrow that God can't comfort. There is no weakness that God can't strengthen. Therefore we all must seek God to heal us of all of our diseases. Our God can heal young African American males from substance abuse. After God heals them, He will sanctify that they may abstain from taking or selling drugs. Our God can take the lust from their beings and fill them with self-love. He can heal families of their co-dependency. God can heal their broken hearts of their guilt and shame. After God heals them, they will no longer feel the need to control, manipulate or condemn drug abusers. They will experience the love of God that will empower them to forgive, let go and let God.

THE HEALING CHURCH

The church should be the place the chains of drug addiction are broken and the people are set free. It should be the place where adolescent, African American males can go to be healed of their paternal deprivation, low self-esteem, drug addiction, inner pain and spiritual slavery. Saints and sinners; drug addicts and drug dealers; the young and the old; and people of all walks of life are welcomed under the umbrella of Christian love, grace and healing. This is what Kenneth Leech meant in his book, Pastoral Care in the Drug Scene. He contends," The theological principle behind the church's involvement in the inner-city crisis is that the drug- taking sub-cultures can only be truly redeemed from within. The churches call therefore, is not to rescue and isolate individual members, but to build within the subcultural groups the structures of spiritual renewal. This is the pattern of incarnation, the self-annihilation of God within the suffering of humanity; only when the grain of wheat dies into the earth does resurrection become possible. The central tasks then is the creation of a community in which if one member suffers all suffer (I. Corinthian 12-26) a community characterized by the sharing of bread and of life (Acts 2:42,44), and this creation is the work of the Spirit, using members of the body. [2] As a caring community coordinated by the love of Christ, we empathize with the suffering and struggles of substance abusers. The drug addict is not an alien but integral part of the family of Christ. Christ is the tie that binds sinner with saint; church with unchurched, drug-free and drug addict. The church is to be a caring community that shares the socio- spiritual brokenness of the substance abuser. The drug-free member assist in the liberation process of the addict. Similarly, the addict aids in the emancipation of the drug-free member enslaved to codependent behavior. The goal is to begin the divine healing process in the family of God, so that everyone moves toward freedom.

READ AND DISCUSS THE FOLLOWING SCRIPTURES:

John 13:34-35 ; Romans 12:9-10 ; Thessalonians 4:9 ; I.Peter 1:22 ; I. John 4:7-8 ; I. John 3:18 ; I. John 4:11 ; Psalm 146:8 ; Matthew 5:44-45 ; Matthew 6:14 ; Luke 6:35-38 ; Romans 12:20

CLOSING PRAYER

LAITY TRAINING SESSION: LIBERATING CHURCH

OPENING PRAYER

SCRIPTURE READING: James 2:5

Historically the Black church has been the vanguard for political, social, economic and spiritual liberation for African American people. The Black church is a voluntary group of African Americans bound together by a kind of psychic- spiritual synthesis resulting from socioeconomic subjugation. Its' referred to as the only establishment owned and controlled by the Black community. This by a large is a true statement. For no other institution other than the church has offered to blacks an opportunity in managing and domineering their destiny other than the Black church. Also, Blacks have had the freedom of developing and refining many of their skills and talents through the Black church. If asked to define the church, most blacks, and especially those without any formal theological training, would define the church as a Body of baptized believers in Jesus Christ. But when asked what the church's mission is, they would most likely respond the mission of the church is to preach the gospel of Jesus Christ to bring humankind into a saving knowledge of Christ which moves the believers to accept the grace of God as manifested in Jesus Christ, thereby experiencing the liberating power of Jesus Christ. However as Olin P. Moyed puts it, "Church and Black religious thought is not merely a doctrine to be debated with regard to authority or relationship to the world. Church in Black religious thought is a psychic- spiritual unity and of a pilgrim people in the process of redemption." [3]

THE CHURCH LIBERATES FAMILIES

This psychic- spiritual interconnection is enhanced by the Black church's sense of family, fellowship, and celebration. Even though African American men and women cherish the family unit, social economic conditions have almost exterminated it. Many Black families have remained stable because the church has served as a reconciliation and redemption center. Drug addiction, dysfunctional families have healed and marital relationships strengthen by the pastoral care and Christian Fellowship. When an African American worshiper makes the statement, "I was glad when they said unto me let us go into the house of the Lord", it has a double meaning for him. It is not only a time of communion with God but is a time of healing fellowship with family and friends. As a place of fellowship with others the Black church is still the center of life for most African Americans. The Black church has never made the sharp distinction between the sacred and the secular. Thus it serves as a social center where friends meet, children are tutored, youth are mentored, the bereaved are comforted, the elderly are assisted, families are strengthened and the addicted are set free. These church activities bring about a sense of healing and liberation for believers and nonbelievers. The church is a place of fellowship that gives meaning and provides the basic ingredient for family stability. It's a place where young African American males can find their surrogate fathers, mentors, uncles, big brothers who will fulfill their paternal deprivation. Moreover the Black church continues to be the vanguard for pursuing racial and social justice .It's a place where the Black community can rally together, organize, protest against social subjugation and pursue political, economic liberation.

WORSHIP AND LIBERATION

The church is a place of worship and celebration. There are three factors that undergird our worship and celebration. First African Americans celebrate the ontological reality of a state of freedom in Jesus Christ. They rejoice in the reality of being justified and thus, being members of the redeemed moving toward the completion of the state of penultimate liberation. Secondly, Blacks extol the corporeality of their survival under insurmountable circumstances of racism which is designed to reduce them into a nonbeing. Thirdly, African Americans laud the hope of future redemptive interventions by God who will eventually redeem God's people from oppression now and in the next life. [4]

WORSHIP CELEBRATION VERSES
RELIGIOUS EMOTIONALISM

Some people inevitably confuse worship celebration and religious emotionalism in the Black worship experience. But they are distinctly different. Religious emotionalism comes from an outside source and is dependent on musical entertainment and theatrical preaching. But worship celebration comes from the anointing of the Holy Spirit. It is not dependent on choirs, praise team, Hammond organs, drums, or oratorical proficiency. The presence of the Holy Spirit is essential to worship celebration. The Holy Spirit moves on believers and touches their heart, mind and soul. Those who worship God in Spirit and in Truth are blessed emotionally, intellectually and socially. Emotionally, they are healed and able to experience His peace and joy. Intellectually, the Holy Spirit gives them wisdom to know the will of God and have a closer walk with God. Finally worship celebration ultimately leads to a more loving, just relationship with others. Worship celebration is motivated by God and for the glory God. Religious emotionalism is motivated by human efforts and for self-glorification. Religious emotionalism changes how you feel, worship celebration changes how you live. Religious emotionalism can lift your spirits, worship celebration can sanctify your soul.

A typical worship service in the Black church will find both religious emotionalism and worship celebration. There are those who attend church for an emotional uplift to pursue their self-centered goals. For them going to church is a network opportunity, a social club with a thin veneer of morality. They go to church not to worship the Lord but to be entertained. They yearn to hear a prosperity gospel or a message that will bolster their fragile self-esteem. But there are those Christian who worship God in spirit and in truth. Their worship celebration becomes a healing experience that brings them closer to God and others.

Our young African American males need to attend churches that promote worship celebration. Religious emotionalism is not going to change their souls. It may make them feel good but it will do them no good. They don't need sweet sermons that pamper their corrupt souls. They need the Bread of Life that will nourish them and empower their liberation process. They need to learn to worship God in Spirit and in Truth. They need a worship celebration that brings healing, and who needs healing any more than those who have experienced the pain and woes of an oppressive society. Worship becomes a therapeutic, liberating experience for many broken hearted impoverished parishioners. Our Lord can set us free every Sunday morning that we may cope with the world's oppression, discrimination and dehumanization.

READ AND DISCUSS THE FOLLOWING SCRIPTURES:

Psalm 100 ; Psalm 95:6-7 ; Psalm 99:9 ; John 4:24 ; Psalm 72:12-13 ; Psalm 107:41 ; Psalm 102:17 ; Psalm 132:15 ; Psalm 68:10 ; Isaiah 11:4

CLOSING PRAYER

LAY TRAINING SESSIONS: BLACK THEOLOGY AND LIBERATION

OPENING PRAYER

SCRIPTURE READING; MATTHEW 25:31-46

Black theology stems from the Black church's sense of family, fellowship and celebration within a context of political, economic, racial, and social bondage. It is from the aspirations of freedom hungry pastors and parishioner that Black Theology of Liberation is developed. It is only through Black Liberation theology that theology can gain any meaningful inroads into the human situation. Theology must communicate to the oppressed, the liberating activities of God. According to Dr. James Cone, a leading Black Theologian, "Christians theology has as its own task the responsibility of analyzing for clarity and communicating the meaning of hope in God in such a fashion that the oppressed will risk all for earthly freedom. Their freedom is made possible through the resurrection of Christ. Christ liberates us from our physical, emotional, and spiritual oppression. The task of Black theology is to discern the nature of the gospel of Jesus Christ in light of marginalized people so they will see the gospel as inseparable from their humiliated condition, bestowing on them the necessary power to break the chains of oppression. This means that Black theology is seeking to interpret the religious dimensions of liberation in the Black community. Black liberation theology provides the basis from which to seek justice and freedom on behalf of the oppressed." [5] It also seeks to deliver souls from spiritual slavery. The God of the Black church is a liberator and a freedom fighter. God frees our souls from the shackles of sins and our bodies from economic exploitation, racial dehumanization, and social subjugation. God saves us from human sin which manifest itself individually and corporately. Individually sin is revealed in immorality, complacency, spiritual alienation, substance abuse and criminality. Social misdeeds manifest themselves in racial and social inequity. It is institutional racism , unjust criminal justice system, substandard public schools, Black unemployment , police brutality that are the social sins that are experienced by African American males on every level. God delivers us from individual and social oppression through the spirit of Jesus Christ. It is the spirit of Christ at work healing and liberating every individual and institution to his glory.

The biblical and theological basis for Christian ministry to young African American males is grounded on the indispensable truth that the God of the oppressed liberates us from sin and social economic injustice. The theme of liberation is the motif for lay ministry among young Black males who are in bondage socially, psychologically, and spiritually. This is a contemporary Christological corrective from the prosperity gospel and secular religion that is practiced today.

The process of liberation involves being delivered out of something into something. Namely, from enslavement to freedom and through freedom into a covenant relationship with God. This is brought to focus in the Old Testament through the following biblical passage," Then the Lord said, I've seen the affliction of my people in Egypt, and have heard their suffering and I've come down to deliver them to a land flowing with milk and honey...." (Exodus 3:7, 8) RVS. In this text, God is aware of the hardship of God's people. God has seen and heard their cry and is come down to rescue them from their bondage. God's aim is freedom for the people of Israel and God uses Moses as God's freedom fighter to bring about this emancipation. God claims Israel as God's own and demonstrates God's desire for their freedom by setting in motion the liberating process through the calling and commission of Moses to lead them out of slavery. Obviously Israel could not experience freedom and remain in Egypt. Thus God delivered them and brought them as free people into a good land where they'll be God's people and their God. In the good land, Israel is to live in a covenant relationship with God. The theme of freedom and community for ministry is clearly focus in the Old Testament. In the New Testament Jesus expresses the purpose for ministry in much the same way. "The spirit of the Lord is upon me because God has anointed me to preach the gospel to the poor. God has sent me to proclaim release to the captives and recovering of sight to the blind, set at liberty those who are oppressed, to proclaim the exceptional year of the Lord."(Luke 4: 18, 19)

It is the spirit of liberation that should permeate the entire church and make it a catalyst for political, economic justice and existential salvation. The nature of the church and the ministry of the laity are in God's emancipation process. It is through the ministry of liberation that young African American males can be set free from social injustice, criminality, slave mentality and drug addiction. It is the church's' moral mandate to do everything in its power to help the least, the lost, and the left out. In Julio De Santa Ana's book, "Towards a Church of the Poor", he writes, "It cannot be the church without the poor present in them. A church without the poor is a place He is obviously left. Therefore, the church should be open to the claims of the poor. It should bear the burden and ask the deprived outside the church and what ways the church can support their cause. As a sign of witness to Jesus Christ, the church must remain attentive to the poor who appeal it. [6] If the church is true to its religious roots, it will seek out ways to alleviate the sufferings of the" endangered species". One of the most deprived, discriminated and destitute of all American citizens is the Black male. He is the victim of high unemployment, homicide, hypertension, incarceration, vilification, drug abuse and a high mortality rate. The church and world will ultimately be judged by whether we have adequately and effectively responded to the exigencies of the Black male and others. The destiny of Black Males is inextricably bound to the destiny of the church. When the house of God fails to respond to them, it fails God. (Matthew 25: 31-46).

READ AND DISCUSS THE FOLLOWING SCRIPTURES:

Matthew 25:31-46 ; James 2:5 ; Psalm 72:12-13 ; Psalm 107:41 ; Psalm 69:33 ; Jeremiah 20:13 ; Psalm 102:17 ; Psalm 113:7 ; Psalm 68:10 ; Isaiah 11:4 ; Isaiah 29:19

CLOSING PRAYER

LAITY TRAINING SESSION: LIBERATING THE SOUL

OPENING PRAYER

SCRIPTURE READING: Romans 6:6-7

The laity are called to emancipate the souls of subjugated youth with the gospel of Jesus Christ. Many young people are addicted to drugs, sexual promiscuity and conspicuous consumerism. The drug culture has tempted them with worldly treasures and fleshly pleasures. The spirituality of the drug culture can be represented in the biblical metaphor of slavery and liberation. Those who are addicted to drugs or alcohol manifests compulsive behavior. They are incapable of refraining from abusing drugs. They are driven by psychological and physiological forces to engage in self-destructive behavior. In a sense, an addict becomes a slave to the drug or alcohol he or she consumes. It is a form of bondage and servitude that will ultimately destroy a person's soul. The New Testament talks about being a spiritual slave to unrighteousness and God's liberation process. Romans 6: 12:13 -16, 17 explain spiritual slavery and freedom this way, "Let not sin therefore reign in your mortal bodies, to make you obey their passions. Do not yield your members to sin as instruments of righteousness. Do you not know that if you yield yourselves to anyone as obedient slaves, you are slaves of the one whom you obey, either of sin, which leads to death, or obedience, which leads to righteousness? But thanks be to God, that you were once slaves of sin have become obedient from the heart to the standard of teaching to which you were committed, and, having been set free from this sins, have become slaves to righteousness." Spiritual slavery can manifests itself in substance abuse, eating disorders, pharisaic legalism, self-idolatry conspicuous consumerism, sexual promiscuity etc. It is the enslavement of the soul to fulfill the lusts of the flesh and one's will is incapable of resisting from engaging in immoral or self-destructive behavior. It is through Christ that we are liberated from our compulsive addictive behavior. He sets us free from any negative feeling, object, person, or behavior that would enslave us. Dr. Sharon Ringe, "Jesus, Liberation and the Biblical Jubilee", points out that," Jesus is the Herald of Liberation who breaks the shackles of individual and social sin. "[7] Only

Christ can free addicts from crack cocaine, alcohol, heroin, and marijuana. Therapy groups may give counsel, console, and challenge codependents and substance abusers. But, they cannot heal, save and liberate the soul like our Lord and Savior Jesus Christ. The laity may use the gospel of Jesus Christ in dealing with the spiritual dimensions of substance abuse. God, in Christ, is no theological abstract or a historical figure. He is a living being, manifesting Himself through the Holy Spirit and liberating us from our compulsive, addictive behaviors. The laity can testify to their own salvation and evangelize young Black males. They will share with them the plan of salvation so that their souls may be free.

READ AND DISCUSS THE FOLLOWING SCRIPTURES:

John 3:16; Romans 10:9,10 ; John 3:3-7 ; I. Timothy 2:3-4 ; Matthew 28:25? ; I. John 2:1-2; II.Corinthians 5:21; Colossians 2:13; I. Timothy 4:9-10; Romans 5:15; Titus 3:4-6;

CLOSING PRAYER

LAITY TRAINING SESSION: LIBERATING THE MIND

OPENING PRAYER

SCRIPTURE READING: Philippians 2: 5-13

The laity have a duty to liberate the adolescent, African American males slave mentality which manifests itself in low self-esteem, violent, aggressive behavior, sexual promiscuity, drug addiction, anti-intellectualism, negative thinking, ungodliness and narcissistic personality disorder. The biblical and theological foundation for the liberation of the mind is largely found in the writings of Paul. Paul articulates how the carnal mind brings about spiritual slavery and death. On the other hand, the spiritual mind is subjected to the laws of God. It leads to eternal life. Romans 8:5-8 records, " Those who live according to the sinful nature have their minds set on what that nature desires but those who live in accordance with the spirit have their minds set on what the Spirit desires. The mind of the sinful man is hostile to God. It does not submit to God's law, nor can it do so. Those controlled by the sinful nature cannot please God."

The slave mentality is also expressed in Philippians 3:19 where it says," Their destiny is destruction, their God is their stomach, and their glory is their shame. Their mind is on earthly things." The earthly mind set of some young Black males needs to be transformed to the mind of Christ. This can only come about by accepting Christ as Lord and Savior and instruction in Christian values, traditions, and principles. Romans 12:1, "Do not conform any longer to the passions of this world, but be transformed by the renewing of your mind. Then you will be able to test and approve what God's will is his good, pleasing and perfect will. "The renewing of young black minds is part of the liberation process. Every time the laity use the word of God to teach our boys they are raising their spiritual conscious level.

The low self-esteem typified by black youths can be eradicated when indoctrinating them with the Scriptures that strengthen their self-perception. Philippians 4:13 records," I can do all things through Christ who strengthens me." Our young boys need to be taught that with God there is nothing they cannot do. They need to be reminded that there are no limits on them except those placed on themselves. They will be encouraged to fulfill their academic goals and professional objectives. The laity will liberate the youth from their poor self-image. They will be instructed not to refer to each other with the "n" word or call women the "b" word. God will break their psychological chains and they will no longer engage in self-destructive behavior .They will discover their divine identity in Christ. They will perceive themselves as children of God, royal priesthood, citizens of the Kingdom of God. They will learn to say like the Psalmist, I am "fearfully and wonderfully made." They will see themselves as God sees them. Consequently, they will no longer lower their pants or their moral standards. They will rise up and be the kind of person God intended them to be. They will have the "mind of Christ" and learn what it is to be a child of God and serve humanity.

The narcissistic personality some adolescent African-American males have can be changed by indoctrinating them with Christian values of service and sacrifice. All throughout Jesus life, he exemplified compassion and service. He fed the hungry, gave water to the thirsty, healed the sick, exercised demons, and preached the gospel to the disinherited. He lived and taught that," It is more blessed to give than to receive." Jesus reminds us that fulfillment comes in a life of service and sacrifice. He liberate us from our own selfish wants and concerns. Philippians 2:3-7 "Do not do nothing out of selfish ambition or vain conceit, but in humility consider others better than yourselves. Each of you should look into not only your own interests, but also to the interests of others. Your attitude should be the same as that of Christ Jesus, being in the very nature, God, did not consider equality with God something to be grasped, but made himself nothing, taking the very nature of a servant, being made in human likeness." The Christian mindset is other centered, otherworldly and positive. The other centeredness is based on the fact that God has given us Jesus Christ and Christ sacrificed himself on the cross. Therefore the foundation of the gospel is the sacrificial life of Jesus Christ who taught, "Deny yourself, take up the cross and follow Him." These are the values that need to be relayed to our self-centered youth consumed in themselves and conspicuous consumerism. They need to be taught how to be a Christian servant and not a drug dealer, thug, and social deviant. They should be taught the shallowness and transitory nature of worldly riches. All of the gold chains, flashy clothes, exorbitant sneakers, and expensive cars and money doesn't determine their self-worth. They need to be instructed in the spiritual dangers of loving money and materialism. I. Timothy 6: 6-10 encourages Christians to have a reasonable perspective on wealth. "But godliness with contentment is great gain. For we brought nothing into the world, and we can take nothing out of it. But, if we have food and clothing, we'll be content with that. People who want to get rich fall into temptation and a trap and into many foolish and harmful desires that plunge men into groaning and destruction. For the love of money is the root of all kinds of evil. Some people, eager for money, wandered from the faith and perceive themselves with many arrows." The laity needs to liberate adolescent African American males from their materialistic mindset that shackles them to worldly treasures. They need to be taught to" lay up their treasures in heaven". Finally, young black males need to understand the folly of drug dealing, stealing, cheating and killing for money. They should realize that there isn't any amount of cash, cars, and clothes worth the price of their souls.

READ AND DISCUSS THE FOLLOWING SCRIPTURES

Ephesians 6:5; Titus 2:9; I. Timothy 6:1; I. Corinthians. 7:20-21; Proverb 23:4-5; I. Timothy 6:17-19; Ezekiel 7:19; Proverb 11:28; Ecclesiastes 5:10; Psalm 41:1

CLOSING PRAYER

LAITY TRAINING SESSION: LIBERATING YOUNG BLACK MAKES WITHIN AN OPPRESSIVE SOCIETY

OPENING PRAYER:

SCRIPTURE READING: Matthew 2: 16

The laity have a duty to liberate young African American males from the social subjugation which manifest itself in unemployment, illiteracy, alienation, self-hatred, addiction, criminal behavior, and high school drop outs. The laity will indoctrinate Black youth in the principles of Ngoro Saba which will serve as a focus for African American personal and collective values, traditions, and cultured experience. It is through these Afro-centric principles that we can eliminate unconscionable degree of self-deprecation and its disastrous social consequences. Our survival and achievements as people is a testimony of the strength, will and proud legacy of African American people.

African American people have overcome overwhelming odds, diabolical oppression by reaching within their roots, customs, culture, and African-based power. We solidify extended family structures, and indomitable faith foundations and a community consciousness that didn't allow anyone to fall through the cracks of society. History is a testimony to the fact before the Civil rights movement, we exhibited the self-determination and sacrifice to create our own businesses, banks, colleges, schools, churches and other institutions .We were able to fight valiantly for justice and brought the hypocrisy out of American democracy. It is all because of the rich legacy of African values and ethics embedded within the African American culture. Therefore, the youth will recapture these African values by practicing the following principles:

1. UMOJA (unity)
2. KUJICHAGULIA (self-determination)
3. UJIMA (collective work and responsibility)
4. UJAMMA (cooperative economics)
5. NIA (purpose)

6. KUUMBA (creativity)

7. IMANI (faith)

These African values will instill in the youth a sense of autonomy and interdependence. They will ultimately lead the youth to a passion for social economic justice. The youth will learn to strive for social and economic independence. Through these principles they will learn how to build a life for themselves their family and the community. They will learn a sense of social responsibility.

Ujima means African unity with God, family, friends, and neighbors. [8] Unity is essential for a sense of well-being and community responsibility. There is an interrelatedness and interdependence in all life. We need each other and should love one another. Unfortunately, racism, classism, sexism and the drug epidemic has divided and destroyed the human family. It has taken a devastating toll on the Black community and particularly on Black males. They have feelings of alienation, which can lead to social deviant behavior. What is desperately needed is a sense of unity among Black males. We must teach our young men that they must have a solidarity based on a fraternity of racial suffering and collective sharing of concern, racial unity and amity.

Kujichagulia means self-determination. [9] It is defined as being responsible for one's own decisions and choices in life. Self-determination means to choose one's own destiny and do all in one's power to fulfill it. It means to have a mind of one's own and not be easily persuaded to do evil. Also, it means to not depend on others for things one can do for oneself. This teaching will destroy the welfare mentality of Black youth. Too many of them believe that the world owes them something. They haven't learned to take pride in themselves and take care of themselves. Kujichagulia principle will get them involved in their own lives and in the community. Black youths will discover how they can take care of themselves and rely on their own God-given gifts and graces. Career counseling will encourage them to go forward in life and leave the street world of drugs, sex, and violence. Furthermore, the Kujichagulia principle will eradicate the disrespect some youths have of themselves and of others.

Self-determination will erase the fatalistic behaviors related to crime, chemical abuse, and sexual promiscuity. It will address those who buy into norms that reflect low self-worth, low self-esteem, and low commitment. They will learn not to accept their neighborhoods blight and decay. They will learn to do what they can to improve their social environment. They will discover what their resources are and use them to improve their living conditions.

Ujima means collective work and responsibility. [10] The laity will instruct youth about the blessings of being industrious and hard-working. The youth will be encouraged to work together on a particular project. They also be encouraged to be more cooperative with their family, friends and neighbors. The youths will be trained not to display flagrant disrespect for elders, men, women and children. They will learn how to respect and appreciate diversity, discipline, sharing, hard work, and faith.

Ujamaa means cooperative economics. [11] The laity will train youth and how to earn money in honest, respectable, creative ways. They will learn the values of making a clean, honest living. Moneymaking projects will be encouraged by the laity with youth. They will understand biblical mandate of being a good steward for God. They will cease from the mindless consumption that makes them kill each other for a pair of sneakers. They need to be taught the work ethic and how they can be prosperous. They need to be encouraged to be self-employed and not just be consumers. African Americans are leading consumers more than other populations. This is not empowering since we don't own the companies. We need to see ourselves as owners not consumers. Our boys should be taught how to make money, save and invest it.

Nia means purpose. [12] The laity will help Black males find meaning and fulfillment in life. The sense of hopelessness will be eradicated by this principle. They will discover who they are and what they can do in life. One of the issues that is critical to young Black males is the poisonous, proliferation of negative images in the media that depicts Black boys as thugs, athletes and entertainers. Therefore, the laity will encourage parents to put strict limits or moratorium on electronic media owned and operated by non- blacks. At the very least, African American families should monitor all broadcasts and limit TV consumption, cell phone use especially for children. The laity will assist the youth to develop a vision for themselves. They will learn how to dream great dreams for themselves and how to pursue them.

Kuumba means creativity. [13] The laity will help adolescent African American males discover their inventive, imaginative, and productive minds. They will be invited to engage in the arts and express their thoughts and feelings. This will allow them to see themselves as creators and not just consumers. Their artistic expressions can be part of the churches worship experience. They will be encouraged to use the rap genre in positive ways. They can rap about God, faith, temptation, love and other positive thoughts. Many of our youth tend to perpetuate Eurocentric norms of beauty, culture and the like. Or there is a tendency to demean some blacks, based on skin pigmentation and hair texture. The youth will learn to appreciate their African features, gifts and talents.

Lastly, Imani means faith. [14] The laity will bolster the faith of young black males. They will be instructed to have faith in themselves, and God and others. They will understand that," Faith is the substance of things hoped for in the evidence of things not seen."(Hebrews 11:1). Faith is believing the unbelievable, conceiving the unconceivable, and achieving the unachievable. Black boys will learn how their faith can enable them to persevere in social injustice and racial discrimination. It means to pursue one's dream in spite of one's nightmare existence.

The indoctrination of these Afrocentric values within adolescent African American males will build self-esteem, community solidarity and be the impetus to social liberation. These principles will cure the internalized oppression that poisons the psyche of African American males. Those who feel threatened by, or who reject, Afrocentricity and do not realize that what they generally regard as normal, "objective" values, language, culture and education are based on Eurocentric norms, and are so narrow, exclusive and distorted that they pose a disadvantage, even for people of European descent. What is needed is an Afrocentric value system which will emphasize collective power toward self-love and Afrocentric affirmation. Our legacy provides the roadmap, our accomplishments sparks the momentum and our current status characterizes the need for urgency.

CLOSING PRAYER

LAITY TRAINING SESSION: PSYCHOLOGICAL BACKGROUND OF YOUNG BLACK DRUG DEALERS

OPENING PRAYER

SCRIPTURE READING: Ephesians 6:1-3

I. DYSFUNCTIONAL BLACK FAMILY

1. NEEDY MOTHER AND SON RELATIONSHIP
    A. CO-DEPENDENT MOTHER
        *Domineering
        *Controlling
        *Manipulative
        *Doesn't hold son accountable
        *Emotionally needy
    B. NARCISSISTIC SON
        *Self-centered
        *Selfish
        *Sexually promiscuous
        *Substance abuser
        *Disrespectful, Argumentative
        *Arrogant, Boastful

II. ABSENT FATHER AND SON RELATIONSHIP

A. WOUNDED FATHER
    *Emotionally absent
    *Physically absent
    *Verbally abusive
    *Physically abusive
    *Lack of interpersonal skills
B. YOUNG BLACK MALE HAS FATHER HUNGER
    *Rebels against mother and "father figures"
    *overachiever, trying to get "fathers approval"
    *underachiever, doesn't feel worthy of being accepted

*Lacks confidence or overly confident

*Searches for a "father figure"

*does not question authority or always question authority

*Bonds with strong criminal figures and or drug dealers

*searches for acceptance with peers or gangs

III. YOUNG BLACK MALE LOW SELF-ESTEEM
1. FALSE BRAVADO AND MACHISMO
2. POOR GRADES, DROP OUT OF HIGH SCHOOL
3. DROP INTO THE DRUG TRADE, MENTORED BY DRUG DEALER, SELLING DRUGS
4. PARTICIPATE IN GANGS
5. BULLY BEHAVIOR, VIOLENCE,
6. SEXUALLY PROMISCUOUS BEHAVIOUR, HAS CHILDREN OUT OF WEDLOCK
7. END UP IN JAIL OR STRUNG OUT ON DRUGS, OR KILLED

CLOSING PRAYER

LAITY TRAINING SESSION: SPIRITUAL BACKGROUND OF YOUNG BLACK MALES

OPENING PRAYER:

SCRIPTURE READING: Acts 13:38

I.   DYSFUNCTIONAL FAMILY
   1.   Mother-son relationship develops a henotheistic faith
   2.   Henotheistic faith develops a life of self-glorification

II.   CO-DEPENDENT CHURCH
   1.   Self-righteous, judgmental members
   2.   Nonexistent or non-relevant youth programs that don't address drug culture
   3.   Nonexistent N.A. or A.A groups
   4.   Irrelevant preaching that does not address drug addiction, gang violence, youth issues
   5.   Ignorance of Youth Culture

III.   MEDIA CORRUPTS THE MORALS AND ETHICS OF OUR YOUTH

   1.   TELEVISION – WATCH
      *violent video games-
      *Family Guy, Jerry Springer
      *movies – "Scarface"
      *Internet
   2.   RAP MUSIC – ASK A YOUTH FOR THE MOST POPULAR RAP SONG AND LISTEN AND DISCUSS IT
      *Lil Wayne
      *Drake
      *Eminem

CLOSING PRAYER

LAITY TRAINING SESSION: YOUNG BLACK MALES AND DRUGS

OPENING PRAYER:

SCRIPTURE READING: ROMANS 6:1, 2

I. WHAT IS MARIJUANA?
    1. It is called cannabis. Its street name is pot, grass, weed, hash, tree or ganga
    2. Its symptoms are red blurry , bloodied eyes , coughing, dry mouth, and hunger
    3. Its harmful effects are disturbed perceptions, impaired coordination, difficulty in problem solving, problems with learning and memory. Marijuana is a gateway drug that leads to other drug addictions.

II. WHAT IS CRACK?
    1. It is a form of cocaine. Crack comes in a rock crystal form that can be heated, inhaled or smoked. It is made with cocaine, baking soda, and ammonia. It is called crack in reference to cracking sound it makes when heated. It has also been called candy, cloud, cookies, crumbs, rock and piece.
    2. Its symptoms are elevated blood pressure, heart rate, temperature, dilated pupils and weight loss.
    3. Its harmful effects are not eating, sleeping , muscle spasms, convulsions, feeling paranoid, hallucinations, severe damage to heart, liver and kidneys, nausea, depression, tooth decay, blistered lips, high blood pressure

III. WHAT IS HEROIN?
    1. Its scientific name is Diamorphine (BAN, INN) and its street name is smack, horse, brown, tar and others.
    2. Its symptoms are constricted (small) pupils, dry mouth, disorientation, droopy appearance, hyper activity followed by nodding off

    3. Those people on heroin will use needles , syringes, burned silver spoons, straws with burn masks, small plastic bags , water pipes

IV. ADDICTIVE PERSONALITY TRAITS
1. Impulsive behavior and difficulty to defer gratification
2. nonconformity
3. sense of social alienation
4. sense of heightened stress
5. lack of self-esteem
6. depression or anxiety

CLOSING PRAYER

LAITY TRAINING SESSION: LIBERATION MINISTRY

OPENING PRAYER

SCRIPTURE READING: MATTHEW 25:31-46

I.   BIBLICAL AND THEOLOGICAL FOUNDATION
  1. Exodus 3:1-10
  2. Luke 4:15-20

II. LIBERATING THE MINDS OF BLACK BOYS
  1. Divine Identity in Christ
  2. Raising self-esteem, "I can do all things through Christ who strengthens me"
  3. Enlighten youth about Black Achievers , pioneers and leaders

III. LIBERATING THE SOULS OF BLACK BOYS
  1. Apostle Paul's concept of Spiritual Slavery and Freedom
  2. Jesus Christ the Liberator
  3. Liberation from drugs, violence, gangs, peers, promiscuity

IV. LIBERATING THE HEARTS OF BLACK BOYS
  1. Learning about the Love of God
  2. Developing a love for God
  3. Developing a love for others
  4. Developing a love for self
  5. Healing the heart

V.   LIBERATING BLACK BOYS SOCIALLY
  1. Kwanza principles
  2. Christian mentoring program
  3. Christian Conflict Resolution Classes

CLOSING PRAYER

LAITY TRAINING SESSION: SOCIAL BACKGROUND OF YOUNG BLACK MALES

OPENING PRAYER:

SCRIPTURE READING: EZEKIEL 34:28

I.   URBAN ENVIRONMENT
1. Crime
2. Unemployment
3. Lack of recreational facilities
4. Drug Culture
5. Gang Activity

II.   PUBLIC SCHOOL FAILURE
1. Pedagogy of the oppressed
2. High school drop out

III.   DRUG CULTURE INDOCTRINATION
1. Scavenger gangs
2. Territorial gangs
3. Drug cartel

CLOSING PRAYER

Chapter Four - End-Notes

1   Hans Kung, The Church, Image Books, Garden City, NY, 1976, p.354.
2   Kenneth Leech, Pastoral Care and the Drug Scene, p.81
3   Olin P. Moyed , Redemption in Black Theology , Judson Press , Valley Forge , PA , 1979 , p. 186.
4   Ibid. p.15
5   James Cone, Black Theology and Liberation, Lippincott, Philadelphia PA, 1970, p.88.
6   Julio De Santa Ana, Towards a Church of the Poor, Geneva: Commission on the Churches Participation in Development, World Council of Churches, p. 1979, p.15.
7   Sharon Ringe, Liberation and the Biblical Jubilee, p.48.
8   Nathan Hare , Bringing the Black Boy to Manhood : The Passage , The Black Think Tank , San Francisco , CA , 1985 , p.12.
9   Ibid.
10 Ibid.
11 Ibid.
12 Ibid.
13 Ibid.
14 Ibid.

Chapter Five

"He has sent me to bind up the brokenhearted, proclaim freedom to the captives and release from darkness for the prisoners." Isaiah 61:1

Liberation Ministries

The training sessions have prepared the laity to conduct the church's' liberation ministries for young African American males. The liberation ministries are designed to break their spiritual, psychological, and social chains. The first liberation ministry is the MY BROTHERS' KEEPER, mentoring program. Its purpose is to liberate their minds from low self-esteem, narcissistic thinking and criminal behavior. The Christian mentoring relationships will fulfill the boys "father-hunger", give them moral guidance and develop them into men of God. The second liberation ministry is the RITES OF PASSAGE PROGRAM. Its goal is to instill Afro-centric values in the boys that will liberate them from the social chains they wear. The young men will develop a sense of purpose and meaning in life. They will be inspired by examples of great African American pioneers, leaders, civil rights workers, scientist, athletes, entertainers, entrepreneurs and over achievers. The third liberation ministry is LIBERATION LESSON SERIES. Its purpose is to raise the spiritual, psychological, and social conscious level of the adolescent African American male through biblical based, youth culturally sensitive lectures and group discussion. These dynamic didactic discussions will develop and liberate their mind and souls to the glory of God. The fourth liberation ministry is LIBERATING LYRICS. We use the lyrics in rap music to teach lessons about what youth should and should not do. We address the spirituality of rap music and its negative values. Also, this is a creative way to get into the world of our youth, discover what their thoughts and feelings are. The adult laity will become educated in youth culture and it will enhance a greater communication between the generations.

MY BROTHERS' KEEPER MENTORING PROGRAM

HOW TO START MENTORING PROGRAM

I. AREAS OF RESEARCH
1. Personally investigate the biblical and theological foundation for laity to minister to youth.
2. Develop a survey and interview the youth in the church to discover their interests and needs.
3. Interview incarcerated young African American male drug dealers to understand their perspective.
4. Interview pastors and lay persons who are currently involved in youth ministry.
5. Investigate all sociological and psychological materials relating to African American males.
6. Personally interview parent(s) who are struggling with their boys.
7. Personally interview community workers about gang and drug activity in the area.
8. Ask youth about their favorite Rap, Hip Hop artist and their music. Listen to their music.

II. CHURCH PLANNING PHASE
1. Develop an Advisory Committee of community workers and concerned persons that will do the research, develop a mission statement, design training sessions, create goals, and plan to utilize the laity in ministry to youth. This committee should be inclusive in gender, age, race, marital status and socio-economic background.

2. Schedule the first meeting of the Advisory Committee and discuss information received from interviews and surveys.

3. Develop a series of training sessions for mentors.

4. Plan for the formation of cadre of mentors consisting of all older African American males who are members of the Church and will consent to a screening process and training sessions.

5. Develop an application for mentors that will entail a screening process(No pedophiles, abusers and people who reject Jesus Christ as Savior)

6. Develop a parental consent form so that boundaries and responsibilities are mutually understood.

7. Schedule dates and an overall agenda for the action components of the project.

8. Develop a plan to reward mentors and workers for participating in "My Brother's Keeper."

III. ACTION PHASE

1. Begin to promote "My Brothers' Keeper" mentoring program via sermons, bible study mass mailings, church announcements and personal invitation. The intent is to recruit mentors and youth workers.

2. Accept applications, interview and screen mentors.

3. Conduct the training sessions with Advisory Committee to equip mentors for ministry. The training lessons should deal with the psychological, spiritual and social background of young Black males. Training sessions should educate laity on Rites of Passage Program, Liberation Lessons, Liberating Lyrics, Conflict Resolution, becoming Peacemaker and understand the healing and liberation foundation of the church.

4. Conduct a meeting with mentors, parent(s) and young boys. At this meeting the mission statement and goals are shared. Also parental consent is signed and mentors are paired up with youth.

5. Establish monthly meetings with mentors, parent(s) and youth for mutual support and additional training.

6. Develop a My Brothers' Keeper Award Ceremony to recognize mentors, volunteers, youth and affirm fulfillment of goals.

The MY BROTHERS' KEEPER MENTORING PROGRAM, requires committed Christian men who will be willing to spend quality time and give moral guidance to adolescent African American youth. They must be trained on spiritual liberation and informed of how racial and social injustice has fragmented the Black family and emasculated the Black male. The high unemployment rate, substandard education, high rates of incarceration and socioeconomic barriers have rendered many Black youth politically impotent, spiritually enslaved, and socially shackled. Moreover, many Black youth have suffered the mental scars of racial oppression and fostered self-hatred. This self-deprecation has led to black on black crime, alienation of self and family. Consequently Black youth are in desperately in need of positive male role models.

Oshersons' book," Finding our Fathers", states that there is a "wounded father" in all men that reflects a paternal deprivation. This wounded father stems from our painful childhood which experienced our fathers as being physically or emotionally absent. The vast majority of black families are headed by single, black women. Absence of fathers in Black families has had a negative psychological effect on some African American males. Their yearning to bond with adult males has led many to seek drug dealers and street thugs as role models. Far too often young boys look up to street hustlers and criminals. It becomes a vicious cycle.

Our young black boys need to know that they can be more than just drug dealers and substance abusers. MY BROTHERS KEEPER MENTORING PROGRAM will give our youth a positive male role model who will help them to grow up to be responsible Christian men. There are several biblical paradigms of male mentoring. Paul was Timothy's mentor. Eli was the protégé of Samuel. Our Lord and Savior Jesus Christ, was a mentor for his disciples. In each example, there was a strong sense of moral responsibility and spiritual bonding. The mentors and the mentees were very committed to one another. There was a sharing and caring within these relationships. In order to be a good Christian Mentor the "TEN MANDATES OF MENTORING" must be adhered to:

TEN MANDATES OF MENTORING

1. The mentor must have a personal relationship with Jesus Christ. He must believe in the death, burial and resurrection of Christ. He must, "confess with his mouth the Lord Jesus and believe in His heart God raised him from the dead. And he shall be saved." (Romans 10:9,10)

2. The mentor must reflect his faith in Christ by the life that He lives. In other words he must have faith that works. He must practice what he preaches. He must , "Let his light so shine among men that they may see his good works and give glory to God."(Matthew 5:13) The mentor must set a good example to the young man.

3. The mentor must believe in the power of prayer. The bible says to "pray without ceasing." They must constantly pray for and with the mentee. The bible says "the prayer of the righteous availed much." The power of prayer can help to transform that wild, young boy into a child of God on fire for the Lord. I have witnessed young people being changed by the power of prayer.

4. The mentor must be led by the Holy Spirit in how he is to interact with the young man. The bible says that the Holy Spirit, "…will guide you into all righteousness." The Holy Spirit will give you the right words to say and the right guidance for the boy's needs.

5. The mentor must be willing to listen non- judgmentally to their boy's thoughts on various topics.

6. The mentor must be willing to honestly share ideas and personal experience (including failures) relative to problems or topics the boy is willing to understand.

7. The mentor must be willing to contact parent or guardian when signs of trouble appear.

8. The mentor must be willing to give spiritual direction.

9. The mentor must be willing to be aware of their own inner emotional need or shortcoming and not project them on to anybody.

10. The mentor must be willing to keep confidentiality with boy. But when there are issues and concerns that may endanger the boy and others the mentor must report it to parent or guardian or

authorities. The mentor must work cooperatively with the pastor and the churches leadership

PURPOSE OF MENTORS

The intent of MY BROTHERS' KEEPER MENTORING PROGRAM is to provide avenues for the discovery of new horizons and a deeper communion with God. The primary purpose of the Christian mentor is to lead young man to a saving knowledge of Jesus Christ. They are to help the boys to understand, that "if they confess with their mouth the Lord Jesus and believe in their heart that God raised him from the dead they will be saved." (Romans 10:9, 10) Also mentoring relationships are based on mutual trust, respect, concern, and collegiality. The Mentors can help develop careers for youngsters based on strong guidance. Mentors can help youth avoid some of life's mistakes and pitfalls. A mentor is an exemplar, coach, role model, teacher, and guide. Mentors don't replace fathers or therapist but support the family structure and not replace it. The mentor must be committed to reach out to their mentee at least four times per month with a visit, or a phone call. The mentor should contact the mentee and find out what is going on in their life. The mentor must be connected to the mentees by developing a rapport with them and encouraging them educationally. The mentor is supposed to be a spiritual support to the youth. Christian Mentors are responsible for making sure that the mentee attend church and be saved, sanctified, and fill with the Holy Ghost. The Christian mentor's primary objective is the salvation and the liberation of his mentee. Mentor can receive his inspiration from the biblical paradigm of Jesus and his disciples. Jesus spent quality time with His disciples. For at least three years he taught them, challenged and comforted them. He showed them how to live by example. He never said or did anything that would discourage or destroy their faith. As Christian Mentors we must follow his example and not quench the spirit of our youth. There are some pitfalls or don'ts of mentoring.

1. Do not make promises you cannot fulfill.
2. Do not do anything without parental consent.
3. Do not involve youth in questionable activities

4. Do not force personal ideologies or philosophies, but be willing to share your faith in Christ.
5. Do not assume too much responsibility.
6. Don't try to change the mentees behavior without establishing a trusting relationship.
7. Don't come to the relationship with a closed mind.
8. Don't set a bad example for the youth

The MY BROTHERS' KEEPER MENTORING PROGRAM conducted at my previous church was a grand success. We were able to lead many boys to a saving knowledge of Jesus Christ and had them baptized! I am of the opinion that this was a great miracle. Some of these boys were ex drug dealers, street runners, and carjackers and high school dropouts. As evil and as wicked as these boys were they were no match for Almighty God. For it was by the power of the Holy Ghost that convicted their hearts and transformed them from sinners to Saints. They used to be slaves of unrighteousness addicted to drugs and alcohol. Now by the grace of God they are slaves of righteousness, servants of God. They were once children of darkness terrorizing the neighborhood and now they are children of light serving the community. It is a miracle to see a young man destined for hell and damnation and now on their way to heaven and glory. It is a miracle to see someone give up drugs, gangs, crime and follow Jesus Christ as Lord and Savior. God really worked miracles through our young people.

Even those who did not accept Christ as Lord and Savior were changed by this program. The unsaved and unchurched boys were taught right from wrong, good from evil. They didn't accept Christ as Lord and Savior but they did decide to give up their evil ways. Many of the boys that were mentored showed a marked improvement in their grades. The mentors were able to give them that extra support they needed so they could excel in school. Moreover some mentors helped their mentees find jobs. They helped them begin to take care of themselves.

MY BROTHERS KEEPER MENTORING PROGRAM was able to be a major support to the single mothers. Many mothers shared their joy and relief that there was someone else who could help them raise their sons. An additional authoritarian voice was all they needed to help their son stay on the right track. In interviews with the boys, it was shared that they were very happy to have male mentors to support them. They liked the idea of getting phone calls and being supported in school and at school activities. They liked having a surrogate father to share their thoughts and feelings with. One young man shared with me how glad he was to see his mentor in the stands as he played football. MY BROTHERS' KEEPER mentoring program fulfilled the paternal deprivation that many of the boys have. It healed the inner wounds that they had and made them learn to respect themselves and others.

MENTOR SUPPORT GROUPS

The MY BROTHERS' KEEPER MENTORING PROGRAM needs a monthly support group to assist the mentors. The mentors need emotional support, guidance and wisdom as they mentor the adolescent African American males. The mentor support groups are an opportunity for the mentors to debrief and share their feelings, thoughts and concerns. Some of the Mentor Support Group meetings were used to problem solve. If there was a difficult situation we were able to discuss it and come up a solution. There were times when a mentor shared how this program got him in touch with his wounded father within. Spending time with the boys reminded them of their boyhood and their absent fathers. Some shared a sense of sadness, anger and alienation toward their fathers. Some recalled bitter experiences they had with their fathers. Others shared how it felt to be demeaned by their domineering fathers. Everyone had the opportunity to share their feelings. It was an opportunity for the mentors to heal and be encouraged in their mentoring. A lot of our deliberations invariably concentrated on their heart wrenching childhood and distant relationship with their fathers. During these times they bonded with each other and strengthened one another. Then there were solemn moments when they reminisced how hurt and humiliated they were by their fathers demeaning diatribes and domineering presence. At times, it seemed as if we were in a therapy group unearthing their passions and vehemence. These meetings allowed the mentors to get in touch with their feelings.

Ultimately, it assisted them to be better mentors and guides for the boys. Once they were in tune to their "inner child", they were more receptive to their mentees. These mentoring meetings disclosed that African American males need a lot of emotional and spiritual subsistence. It seems as if the mentoring program opened a Pandora's Box of African American male misery and chagrin. They have a lot of psychological and spiritual extremities. Mentoring program scratched the surface and exposed their indecencies. Some of the men admitted they weren't willing to share their personal feelings for fear of losing moral credibility. One mentor said," If I told my boy what I used to do when I was their age they'd never listen to a word I say". Some of the mentors shared that they had to contact with the parents because of unruly, disrespectful, behavior. There was one mentor who ruined his relationship with the youth because of his rigid authoritarianism. The youth rebelled against him because he felt suppressed by the mentors domineering presence and direction. This mentor learned that he needed to develop a trust level before he challenged the boy. All of the mentors tried to emphasize the indispensable necessity of keeping in touch with the boys until they graduated and made a contribution in society. They all shared the commitment to educational excellence.

RITES OF PASSAGE PROGRAM

"Dark am I, yet lovely, O daughters of Jerusalem, dark like the tents of Kedar, like the tent curtains of Solomon."
Song of Songs 1:5

The Rites of Passage Program for adolescent African American males will raise their self-esteem and develop their sense of social responsibility. It is based on the Afrocentric principles of Nguzo Saba or Kwanza which serve as a focus for African American collective value, traditions and cultured experience. They emphasize collective power towards self-love, Afrocentric affirmation and social liberation. The Rights of Passage are Umoja (unity), Kujichagulia (self-determination), Ujima (collective work and responsibility), Ujamma (cooperative economics), Nia (purpose), Kuumba (creativity) and Imani (faith). The laity will assist the adolescent African American males in the fulfilling of each of these principles in their lives. The youth will have to demonstrate their understanding of these principals by engaging in a community projects. Once the youth have fulfilled each of the principles they will have matriculated from boyhood to manhood; from slavery to liberation. An award ceremony can be given as the boys fulfill all their requirements in the Rites of Passage program.

UMOJA

The first step in the Rites of Passage is Umoja. The laity must teach the boys the meaning of unity in the home, school, amongst peers and on the street. They must learn the concept of team work as it relates to their everyday lives. There are several ways that the boys can reveal Umoja.

1. Write a two page essay on how you will show Umoja in the home , school , among peers and enemies
2. Do a community outreach project with someone or a group of people
3. Try to be a peace maker and get opposing people to talk with one another
4. Reach out and reconcile with your biological father

5. End arguments and fights in the home or in school
6. Share your thoughts, feelings , talent , time or resources with someone to create harmony
7. Reach out to someone who appears to be isolated, withdrawn or friendless.

KUJICHAGULIA

The second step in the Rites of Passage is Kujichagulia which means self-determination. The laity must instruct the youth on the meaning of self-determination. Self-determination is a necessary requirement for success in any endeavor. It means not to give up or quit. It means to hang on in there no matter what the odds or obstacles. The following are some suggested ways the laity can assist the youth in fulfilling Kujichagulia.

1. Write a two page typed essay on how you will reveal Kujichagulia in home, school, among peers
2. Do a community outreach project that requires a lot of hard work, patience and persistence.
3. Be willing to break from bad relationships with peers, gangs and drug dealers who have negatively influenced your life.
4. Show determination in working hard to improve your grades and not dropping out of school.
5. Show your determination in pursuing getting a job and not quitting it.

UJIMI

The third step in the Rites of Passage is UJimi or collective work and responsibility. The laity will instruct the youth in learning how to work with others. The youth must understand that they can accomplish more with others than being alone. This will challenge the narcissistic mind set of the adolescent African American male. They must learn that this is not their world. Therefore the following projects are suggested:

1. Write a two page essay on Ujima as it relates to family, school and peers.

2. Develop an outreach project that requires you to work with someone who can hold you accountable for the work that you have done.

3. Volunteer to work with others at a homeless shelter or nursing home

UJAMMA

The fourth step in the Rites of Passage is Ujamma and that is cooperative economics. The laity will teach the youth the value of money, work ethic, business principals, investments, budgets and prosperity. Cooperative economics is a corrective to the lucrative drug trade that tempts our children and youth. Ujamma can be manifested in the following ways:

1. Write a two page typed essay on how Ujamma differs from the drug trade.

2. Ask your parent(s) if you can develop a budget with them and assist them in the paying of bills

3. Develop small business that has little or no overhead and can bring in a profit

4. Interview someone who manages a business and meet with them once a week for at least a month. Write a journal about everything you learned

5. Get a job and learn how to save and budget your money

6. Get someone you trust to put your money together to invest in business together

7. Ask someone how to develop a budget and a business plan

NIA

The last step in the Rites of Passage is the principal NIA and it means purpose. The laity will assist the youth in developing a purpose or vision for their life. A personal vision is critical to a person having a sense of fulfillment and success in this life. So often our youth lack a positive vision for their lives and they end up fulfilling the negative images and stereotypes that the world projects on them. There is a major problem when the only vision that our youth have for themselves is the neighborhood thug or drug dealer. Our youth must envision a more positive image of themselves. The laity will work with the youth to fulfill Nia in the following ways:

1. Write a two page typed essay on your vision in life and the way you will go about achieving it.
2. Seek out a mentor in the field that you want to pursue and interview him.
3. Go to the office or institution of the profession that you want to pursue and observe what everyone does and record it and write a two page typed paper
4. Read the biography or autobiography of a famous African American and write a two page paper summarizing their life and the lessons you learned and how it applies to you.

The Rites of Passage will develop the youth's self-esteem, their ability to work with others, there sense of self-determination, their financial acumen and their purpose in life. One way to encourage the boys is to give them a certificate as they complete each of the step. The certificates can be given in worship service, in Sunday school class, at Mission meeting, in Youth group meetings or at a family gathering. This will bolster their self-esteem and affirm their learning in the presence of others. A banquet could be held at the end of the Rites of Passage program and awards given for those who finished. This will be a grand celebration for the youth, their family and the church. They will be able to celebrate the fact that their boy became a man and the slave was set free.

LIBERATION LESSON

"Young man, I say to you, get up!" Luke 7:14

The Liberation lesson series will raise the spiritual, psychological and social conscious level of young African American males. Every week the laity can speak to the boys on various youth issues from a biblical, spiritual perspective. The lesson will be followed up by a group discussion that will enable the youth to reflect on their lives and take progressive actions toward their own liberation. The objective of the group discussion is to bring about the liberation process of the mind, soul and heart of the youth.

It is the laity's' responsibility to liberate young Black males. They are called to emancipate the souls of oppressed youth with these liberation lesson. Many young people are enslaved to marijuana, cocaine, heroin and alcohol. The drugs have captivated them to strong psychological and physiological passions that have made them self-destructive. They have become spiritual slaves and the only one that can free them is Jesus Christ. Our Lord and Savior is strong enough to break their psychological and social chains. The liberation lessons will give the laity the opportunity to introduce Jesus Christ to the youth and give them the opportunity to be free.

It is the laity's' task to free the young Black males from their slave mentality that is revealed in their poor self-image, drug addiction, overly aggressive behavior, narcissistic thinking and ungodly perspective. Each liberation lesson is designed to address one of these issues. Ultimately these lessons will "…transform and renew their minds." (Romans 12:2) The renewing of young Black minds is part of their liberation process. As a result of hearing these lessons and participating in the group discussion, they will be set free from their self-hatred, negative thinking, self-centeredness, addictive behavior and worldly wickedness.

Also, these liberation lessons can be used by parents as they spend quality time teaching their sons. Every parent has a spiritual responsibility to teach their children about God, the Holy Bible and the will of God. A parent's primary purpose in life is to instruct their children about the Lord Jesus

Christ and learn how to have a personal relationship with Him. Moreover parents must teach their children how to discern good from evil and right from wrong. These liberation lessons are a perfect tool for parents to teach the basics of the Christian faith in an idiom they can relate to. Personally, I have used these lessons to teach my son and they have been effective. My son enjoyed reading some of them and learned some things in the process. Also the questions at the end of the lessons provided some interesting and enlightening discussions.

LIBERATION LESSON: FROM SLAVERY TO LIBERATION

OPENING PRAYER

SCRIPTURE: Romans 6:17

The Bible states," Thanks be to God that, though you used to be slaves to sin, you wholeheartedly obey the form of teaching to which you were entrusted. You have been set free from sin and have become slaves to righteousness."(Romans 6: 17,) A slave to sin is someone who cannot control their fleshly passions and worldly desires. They are addicted to someone, something, some feeling or some experience. A slave to sin lacks the self-discipline and self-restraint to refrain from doing evil. As Shelley put it," All spirits are enslaved which serve things evil." You can be enslaved or addicted to drugs, alcohol, money, clothes, food, cigarettes, gambling, violence or anything you are dependent on. There are many teens who are addicted to drugs. They love the high they get from it and can't refrain from it. Only Jesus Christ can liberate us from our addictive behaviors and set us free from drugs, alcohol, sex, etc. Jesus said, "You will know the truth and a truth will set you free" (John 8:32).

1. What is the truth about yourself? Have you ever been "high" before and what was it like?
2. Do you know anyone who is an addict? How do they act?
3. Are you an addict? Why or why not?
4. Can someone be addicted to marijuana? Why or why not?
5. Why is drug use bad for you?
6. Why is selling drugs bad for you and the community?
7. How is being a drug user like being a slave?
8. Do you believe that Jesus Christ has the power to set you free from your addictions?
9. Are you willing to accept the fact that only Jesus Christ can set you free from drugs?

CLOSING PRAYER

LIBERATION LESSON: BLACKS IN THE BIBLE

OPENING PRAYER

SCRIPTURE: Genesis 10

The African Egyptians permeated the entire Bible and largely influenced the thought of Christian theology. Before the Old Testament was written an African Egyptian Pharaoh named Akhenaton developed the belief of monotheism which is the belief in one supreme God. Moses developed this thought and called it Yahwism and promoted it among the Jewish people. As Acts 7:22 states, "And Moses was learned in all the wisdom of the Egyptians." The biblical support to the physical presence of Blacks in the Old Testament can be found in Genesis 10: 6 "The sons of Ham were Cush, Mizoram, Phut, and Canaan." Ham colonized an area of North Africa designated by the Bible as the land of Ham. First born Cush forged his way inland and established the Cushite's. Their dark skin color identified them with the people who had colonized Egypt. Other scriptures referring to Blacks in Old Testament are:

- Queen of Sheba or Makeda – I.Kings 3:1 & II. Chronicles 9:9
- Cushite in David's Army – II.Samuel 18:21
- Joseph married an African woman – Genesis 41:44
- Jethro , Josephs father-in-law was an Ethiopian priest – Exodus 18:41
- Other Old Testament scriptures Psalm 105:23 ; 106:21-22 ; 78:51 ; Jer. 13:23, Judges 4:11

In the New Testament there are several Blacks who are mentioned. Apostle Paul had five prophets who were involved in his ordination, two were black Africans. They were Simeon called Niger and Lucius of Cyrene (Acts 13: 1-3). Among Jesus 12 disciples, Simon the Canaanite was a descendent of Ham, the father of Canaan (Matthew 10:1-4 and Luke 6: 12-16) Another Simon, the Cyrenian, was Black and helped Jesus carry the cross (Luke 23:26). An Ethiopian eunuch was converted to the gospel (Acts 8:27).

Jesus' great, great grandmother Rehab the prostitute was a Canaanite from North Africa. (Matthew 2) Therefore Jesus himself had African roots.

1. Did you think that all of the people in the bible were white?
2. God was working through Africans in the Old Testament and New Testament. What does that say about God?
3. Do you believe that God is a respecter of no one and will use you to his glory?
4. How has God worked through you?
5. What do you think about the fact that Jesus, great, grandmother was African? Does that change the way you think of Him or yourself?
6. God sees everyone as his child and refers to all people as His children. Why do some African Americans refer to themselves and others with the "N" word?
7. Is the "N" word offensive to you why or why not?
8. Would you refer to your mother or Jesus with the "N" word? Why or why not?

CLOSING PRAYER

LIBERATION LESSON: FAITH

OPENING PRAYER

SCRIPTURE: Hebrews 11:1,2

Jesus Christ once said, "I tell you the truth, if you have faith as small as a mustard seed, you can say to this mountain, move from here to there and it will move. Nothing will be impossible for you."(Matthew 17:20). When Almighty God created us, he put a mustard seed of greatness into our nature. As a child of God you have unlimited potential to achieve many great things. It is your faith in God that will enable you to move any mountain, overcome any obstacle and transcend any tragedy. You may not have a lot of talent, skills, money, resources or educational degrees. But if you have faith you still can achieve the impossible. Thomas Edison said, "If we did all the things were capable of doing we would literally astound ourselves." You will amaze yourself when you start believing in yourself and God. There is nothing you can't do. But you must never lose faith in yourself and in God.

1. What do you want to be when you grow up and why?
2. Do you believe in yourself? Why or why not?
3. Have you ever felt inadequate at school, home, amongst friends or doing something new?
4. What do you do when you are confronted with a problem? Do you give up? Do you pretend there is no problem? Do you make excuses? Do you believe in God and attempt to solve it?
5. Describe a "mountain" in your life and how you handle it.
6. Do you have faith to climb your mountain?
7. Do you have faith to tunnel through your mountain?
8. What kind of self-esteem do you have?
9. What kind of faith does a winner have?
10. How can your faith improve your grades?
11. How can your faith determine your career?

CLOSING PRAYER

LIBERATION LESSON: BLACK ACHIEVERS & INVENTORS

OPENING PRAYER

Every February we celebrate Black history month. But we should not wait till February to acknowledge and recognize the great contributions and achievements of African Americans. Our ancestors were able to overcome obstacles, rise above racism, and transcend poverty. Through their perseverance all Americans have benefited. We cannot begin to list all of the achievements and feats of African Americans. What is remarkable about all of these courageous creators is that they never gave up on themselves and their dreams. An African proverb says it better," The African race is like an Indian rubber ball. The harder you bounce it to the ground, the higher it will rise." The following inventions were created by African Americans:

- Burglar Alarm, TV Tubes, Alexander Louis
- Traffic Signal , Garrett A. Morgan
- Sugar (1843) , Norbert Rillieux
- First Open Heart Surgery, Daniel Hale Williams
- Guitar (1886) , R.F. Fleming
- Refrigerator (1881) Lewis Latimer
- Lawn Mower (5-9-1899) , J.A.Burr
- Air Conditioning Unit (7-12-49) F.M. Jones
- Pencil Sharpener (11-23-1897), J.L.Love
- Fire Extinguisher (5-26-1872) J.J.Marshall
- Fountain Pen (1-7-1890) W.B. Purvis
- Brush (4-15-1898) L.D. Newman
- Lawn Sprinkler (5-4-1897) J.W.Smith
- Clock (1804) Benjamin Banneker
- Discovered Chicago (1745-1818) Jean Baptiste Pointe Du Sable "Blacks in Science", by Hattie Caldwell and "1999 Facts about Blacks", by Raymond Corbin

1. Did you realize that African Americans created and did so much for this country?

2. What Black invention have you used?
3. Did you ever think of yourself as an inventor or a creator? Why or why not?
4. If you could not be an entertainer or athlete what would you like to be? Why ?
5. What qualities does it take to be successful?
6. The earlier inventors had very little resources, educational degrees yet they were able to do great things. What does that say to us?
7. Are you inspired by their example? Why or why not?
8. What can you learn from these great achievers and pioneers?

CLOSING PRAYER

LIBERATION LESSON: DRUGS, ALCHOHAL, AND THE BIBLE

OPENING PRAYER

SCRIPTURE: Proverbs 23:29-35

The Bible states," Do not get drunk on wine, which leads to debauchery. Instead, be filled with the Spirit."(Ephesians 5:18). According to the scriptures all drugs and alcohol abuse for worldly pleasure can lead to immorality and spiritual slavery (I. Corinthians 5:11, Proverbs 23: 29-35, Isaiah 28: 7-8). Jesus Christ warns "Be sober or your hearts will be weighed down with drunkenness…(Luke 21:34). Getting high or drunk can lead to becoming an addict , a high school dropout, unemployed, criminal behavior, sexual promiscuity, divisions in the family, and broken hearts. Unfortunately we ignore the Bible warning. Two- thirds of U.S. population drink alcohol, 68% use marijuana, 5 million use cocaine, one-half million use heroin and 20% use stimulants, sedatives for non-medical purposes (Jones, p.385). We are slowly become a nation of addicts.

1. Why do you think people use drugs and alcohol?
2. What are some of the symptoms of being an addict?
3. Have you ever tried marijuana and what was it like?
4. Have you ever tried crack or cocaine and what was it like?
5. Have you tried heroin and what is it like?
6. How do you know if you are an addict or not?
7. What can you say and do for an addict?
8. Have you given your life over totally to Jesus Christ?
9. Did you know that Jesus Christ can deliver you from addiction?
10. Do you have friends who sell or use drugs? What could you say to them?
11. If you continue to hang around them what do you think could happen?(Proverbs 23:21)

CLOSING PRAYER

LIBERATION LESSON: UMOJA

OPENING PRAYER

The Kwanza principle Umoja means unity with God, friends, and self. There is an interrelatedness and interdependence to all life. We need and depend on one another.

1. How is the drug dealer dividing our community?
2. What could you do to bring unity to the community?
3. What could you do to bring unity in your family?
4. What could you do to be unified with God?
5. How can you be a peacemaker?
6. What can you do to put an end to the guns and violence in the community?

CLOSING PRAYER

LIBERATION LESSON: KUJICHAGULIA
(pronounced coogeekageela)

OPENING PRAYER

The Kwanza principle Kujichagulia means self-determination. It means to be responsible for your own decisions and destiny. It means to take care of yourself and realize your own gifts and graces.

1. In what ways are you taking care of yourself physically?
2. In what ways are you taking care of yourself emotionally?
3. In what ways are you taking care of yourself spiritually?
4. Are you using your talents and skills to take care of yourself?
5. How does taking drugs destroy your self-determination?
6. How does selling drugs destroy other people's right to self-determination?

CLOSING PRAYER

LIBERATION LESSON: JUIMA (pronounced You-gee-ma)

OPENING PRAYER

The Kwanza principle Juima translates to collective work and responsibility. This value emphasizes hard work with others. It also focuses on self-discipline, respecting others and sharing.

1. What can you do to work well with others?
2. What do you say or do that prevents you from working well with others?
3. What could you say or do to work with the police and others to stop crime in the community?
4. Do you use derogatory, racist words to describe Black people? Why or why not?
5. Do you use derogatory, sexist words to describe woman? Why or why not?

CLOSING PRAYER

LIBERATION LESSON: UJAMMA
(pronounced You-ja-ma)

OPENING PRAYER

The African principle Ujamma is translated to mean cooperative economics. This focuses on making a clean, honest living. It points out the value of money and being a good steward of it.

1. How can you earn money without selling drugs?
2. Have you saved any money? Why or why not?
3. What could you do to earn money in a legitimate way?
4. Why is it wrong to sell drugs?
5. Why is it wrong to buy drugs?
6. What could you say or do to end the drug trade in the community?

CLOSING PRAYER

LIBERATION LESSON: NIA (pronounced Nee-A)

OPENING PRAYER

The kwanza principle NIA translates to purpose or meaning in life. It means to have a sense of direction and knowing yourself. It means having a vision or purpose in life.

1. What do you want to be in life and why?
2. What kind of life do you think drug dealers or users have?
3. What kind of grades do you want and what specific things are you doing to ensure it?
4. What is your vision for your family and what can you do to make it happen?
5. The bible says, "Where there is no vision the people perish." What does that mean?
6. The bible says, "Write the vision and make it plain." Write out the vision for your life.

CLOSING PRAYER

LIBERATION LESSON: KUUMBA (pronounced coomba)

OPENING PRAYER

The Kwanza principle KUUMBA translates to creativity. You should be able to creatively express your thoughts and ideas through the arts, language and by being yourself.

1. Are you trying to be someone else? What makes you unique or different?
2. What are your gifts, talents, skills and in what ways do you use them?
3. There is some rap music that is demeaning to women. Can you name a song and recite the lyrics?
4. Why do you think rappers use racial derogatory terms to describe Black people?
5. Why do you think some rap artist use sexist derogatory words to describe women?
6. There are some artist and entertainers who sell their creativity by using sexual images. Is this right? Why or why not?
7. Create your own rap song and use positive lyrics.

CLOSING PRAYER

LIBERATION LESSON: IMANI
(pronounced ee-mon-knee)

OPENING PRAYER

The Kwanza principle IMANI translates to faith. You should have faith in God, yourself, and others. Faith is believing in yourself no matter what people say about you. It means to never give up on your dreams and goals.

1. How will your faith help you to get through school?
2. Does a person who has faith need drugs or alcohol? Explain.
3. How will your faith in Christ help you?
4. How can your faith in God empower you not to get high or drunk?
5. Faith means working, sacrificing, studying hard and fighting for your dreams. In what ways is your faith pursuing your dreams?

CLOSING PRAYER

LIBERATION LESSON: BELIEF IN GOD AND YOURSELF

MEDITATION

A weak and frail Christian preacher named Paul who was faced with a lot of adversity and affliction in life wrote these powerful words, "I can do all things through Christ who strengthens me." Paul had an unconquerable belief in himself and in God. What about you? Do you believe in yourself or do you doubt yourself? Life's difficulties have a way of knocking us down and filling us with self-doubt. What makes it worse is, that there are cruel people, who will kick us when we are down. We may even criticize and condemn ourselves. But you must resist this masochistic temptation and express your belief in God and yourself. When others say you can't do something, you must say like Paul, "I can do all things through Christ who strengthens me." When you are striving to improve yourself; struggling against an addiction or pursuing your dream tell yourself, "I can do all things through Christ who strengthens me."

1. What do you have doubts about and why?
2. How can your belief in God help you to fulfill your dreams?
3. How can your belief in God help you in doing well in school?
4. How can your belief in God help you to live right?
5. How can your belief in God help you from getting high or drunk?

CLOSING PRAYER

LIBERATION LESSON: SEXUAL PROMISCUITY

OPENING PRAYER

MEDITATION

The Bible says, "The wages of sin is death but the gift of God is eternal life through Jesus Christ our Lord". (Romans 6:23) When we practice sexual sins like pornography, voyeurism, promiscuity, homosexuality, adultery, and fornication we put our souls in jeopardy. (Matthew 5: 27, 28, I. Corinthians 6:12- 20; II. Peter to 2:4-10; I. Thessalonians 4:3-6) Sexual promiscuity is not only injurious to the soul but also the body. The venereal diseases, HIV (human immunodeficiency virus) and AIDS (acquired immune deficiency syndrome) can be contracted through sexual sins. Around the world, estimated 8 million to 10 million people are infected with HIV. The spread of AIDS is especially rapid in Asia, Latin America, and Africa. Nationally, Blacks make up about 12.5% of the population, but they represent 29% of all reported cases of AIDS. In Michigan Blacks make up 14% of the population but a startling 48% of AIDS cases. There are more than 3 thousand cases reported in Michigan to date. Hundreds of new AIDS cases were reported in the past year came from heterosexual contact. AIDS can also be transmitted through contaminated syringe needles, blood transfusions, mothers can infect fetuses, and homosexual contact. Some AIDS-related symptoms are toxoplasmosis which is lesions in brain, lungs, heart; candida albicans which is fungal growth found in mouth, brain, and spinal cord; kaposis sarcoma a skin cancer; pneumocystis carinil pneumonia which is a persistent cough and fever. The AIDS virus is capable of entering the blood cells and killing people. Presently, there is no protection against invading bacteria, viruses, or fungi. Current statistics show 50% of those with HIV will have AIDS within 10 years.

1. Do you think sex outside of the context of marriage is a sin? Why or why not?
2. Abstinence is the will of God. Are you willing to abstain from sexual activity? Why or why not?

3. Do you think that you can tell if a girl has a sexually transmitted disease by her looks?
4. What is safe sex and do you practice it?
5. The bible teaches us not to have sex until we are married. What do you think?
6. Do you believe that God can give you the inner strength to refrain from having sex?
7. Are you willing to take care of a baby?
8. What do you think about the statement, "Any boy can have a child. It takes a man to raise a child."
9. The bible says homosexuality is a sin. What do you think and why?
10. Do you respect girls that you see the same way you treat your mother or sister? Why?
11. What are the sexist words used to refer to women? Why is it wrong to use these words?
12. What do you think of strippers and prostitutes? What does God think of them?

CLOSING PRAYER

LIBERATION LESSON: HE'S GOT YOUR BACK

OPENING PRAYER

MEDITATION

The Psalmist boldly proclaimed, "The Lord is my Light and My Salvation, whom shall I fear. The Lord is the strength of my Life of whom shall I be afraid?" (Psalm 27:1, 2) It took a lot of faith and courage for the Psalmist to make this statement. He was facing a gang of men who were trying to kill him. King Saul wanted him dead and sent his soldiers after him. In spite of death threats, the Psalmist had faith that God would take care of him. He knew God had his back.

As a young man being raised in a violent society you may have feared for your life. Maybe there is someone who has threatened to beat you up. There maybe someone who has verbally abused you and even threatened to do your family bodily harm. Or it may be a rival gang is out to get you. Or maybe someone in your own family or in school is bullying you.

If you feel intimidated or afraid, remember that the Lord has your back. He is with you. His powerful presence will give you the courage to confront your enemies .He is your Light and you be able to see thru the darkness of your fears. You will be able to see that your enemies can only touch your body and not your soul. They cannot change who your really are and what your all about. They cannot make you do something you do not want to do. They cannot make you feel afraid unless you let them. You don't have to fear anyone. The Lord has your back. He will not abandoned you or forsake you. He will give your courage and strength. He has your back.

1. Who or what are you afraid of?
2. Have you ever been bullied? What happened and how did you feel?
3. Are you a bully? Do you intimidate people? Do you like being in charge, always having your way and telling others what to do? If so, what could you do to change?
4. Why is it bad to bully people?

5. How can the Lord help you with a bully? Have told someone about this bully?

*You can have faith in the Lord in spite of your fears and not let anyone intimidate you.

CLOSING PRAYER

Dr. Samuel White, III

LIBERATION LESSON: YOLO

OPENING PRAYER

MEDITATION

The bible instructs us, "Teach us to number our days, that we may have a heart of wisdom." The scriptures give us a sobering reminder that life is short. The older you get the more you realize that you do not have a lot of time. Those of you who are in your teens or twenty's may think you have a lot of time. But just because you are young does not mean you cannot die young. Death is democratic and surrendipidus. It will take who it wants, when it wants, and how it wants. Many young people get killed every day. The reality of death reminds us that YOLO --"YOU ONLY LIVE ONCE." Every day is gift from God and should be cherished and appreciated. Every day that you get up in the morning is an opportunity to live right and do right. Every hour that you have is a privilege to show your family how much you love them. Every second that you are blessed with is a chance for you to express your gratitude to God. So live your life to the fullest. Pursue your passion. Make your dreams come true. YOLO!!

1. If you knew you were going to die in the next 6 months, what would you do differently?
2. Why not live your life as if there is no tomorrow?
3. Do you know of any teenager or young person who died? How do you feel about it? If they were alive would they tell you YOLO? Why or why not?
4. Is getting high, having sex, selling drugs or engaging in other criminal activity practicing YOLO? Why or why not?
5. If God told you, YOLO. What do you think He wants you to do?

CLOSING PRAYER

LIBERATION LESSON: STARTED FROM THE BOTTOM

OPENING PRAYER

MEDITATION

The Superstar Rapper, Drake sings, "It started from the bottom, now we are here. Started from the bottom now the whole team is here." If you overlook all the profanity in the song there is a great message. Drake proudly sings about his being able to rise from obscurity to be a mega superstar. The basic message of the song is that everyone can begin from humble beginnings, work hard and be a great success in life. There is nothing wrong starting from the bottom. Many people are born and raised in abject poverty. There are those who are at the bottom academically. They are "D" students who are one test score from dropping out of school. There are those at the bottom spiritually. They are addicted to drugs or alcohol. They live immoral lives and may have had a run-in with the law. There are those at the bottom emotionally. They are always sad, depressed or angry in life.

No matter where you are in life, you don't have to stay there. You may have started from the bottom but you can study, work, struggle, fight and even crawl your way to the top. There is nothing and no one that can stop you unless you let them. There is something about the human spirit that cannot be broken or denied. Our African American fore parents started from the bottom. They were treated as beast of burden, three-fifths of a person, second class citizens and yet they became inventors, pioneers, freedom fighters, entrepreneurs, athletes, medical doctors, lawyers, nurses, entertainers and many other things. They did not own any property, have any resources, had little or no formal education, no political power or prosperity. Yet out of a bottomless vitality they were able to establish their own colleges, start their own business', build their own churches, own their own banks, elect their own leaders and establish their own communities. We started from the bottom and now we are here. We are here in every profession, privileged position and post of power. And the fact that there is an African American President in the White House reveals that we started from the bottom and now we are here!

1. What is your bottom? How do you feel about it?
2. How is God helping you to deal with your bottom?
3. What do you have to do to rise up from the bottom?

CLOSING PRAYER

LIBERATION LESSON: HAPPINESS

OPENING PRAYER

MEDITATION

Hip-hop superstar, Pharrell Williams' sings, "Clap along if you feel like a room without a roof. Because I am happy. Clap along if you feel like happiness is the truth. Because I am happy. Clap along if you know what happiness is to you. Because I am happy." Happiness is something that everyone wants but few really have. Many people pursue happiness in many different ways. Some pursue happiness in getting high or drunk. But that ends up in a hangover or hunger pains. Some seek happiness in sexual conquest. But sexual relationships often reveal a deep hole in the heart. Some pursue happiness by buying things and having a lot of money or property. But the treasures of this world cannot satisfy the soul.

The only way we can be happy is through a personal relationship with Jesus Christ. True happiness comes from within. Jesus said, "You have my joy and your joy maybe full." The joy of Jesus is fundamentally different from the happiness of the world. The happiness of the world is material, the joy of Jesus is spiritual. The happiness of the world cost money, the joy of Jesus cost the cross. The happiness in the world stems from the flesh, the joy of Jesus stems from the Spirit. The happiness of the world ultimately leads to damnation, the joy of Jesus ultimately leads to salvation. Which one would you rather have, the worlds' happiness or the joy of Jesus?

1. Are you happy? Why or why not?
2. Do you have a personal relationship with Jesus Christ?
3. What could you do to be happier?
4. What makes you sad?
5. The joy of Jesus can only be experienced with a personal relationship with Him, focusing on Him and counting your blessings. How often do you count your blessings?

CLOSING PRAYER

LIBERATION LESSON: YOU CAN BE GREAT

OPENING PRAYER

MEDITATION

Jesus told two highly competitive brothers, "He who is greatest among you, will be a servant. And he who would be first must be last." (Mark 10:35-44) The two brothers name were James and John. They were competing and arguing with one another about who would be first in Gods' kingdom. They both wanted to rule and be in charge. They both wanted to be great.

The desire to be great, to be supreme is an innate quality in human beings. Many people are fierce competitors and would do almost anything to be number one. This is especially true amongst some young African American males. Many of the killings in the ghetto occur because of two young men fighting for respect. Some of the gang related killings are due to power and prosperity. Far too many young Black males think that greatness comes through having a lot of guns, money, property and women. They think greatness comes from being served, adored, worshipped, feared and followed.

But our Lord teaches us the complete opposite. True greatness has nothing to do with the car your drive, the size of your home, the money you possess or the bling, bling you wear. According to Jesus, those persons who are truly great are servants of others. In the eyes of God, the givers not the takers are great. The more a person sacrifices and struggles on behalf of others the greater they become. Therefore the young African American male who shares his belongings is greater than the one who brags about his designer glasses, and $200 sneakers. The teenager who helps an elderly person cross the street is greater than the one cruising in a Cadillac escalade. The Black male who turns the other cheek is greater than the one packing a Saturday night special. So if you really want to be great in the eyes of God, help someone in need. For it is in your service to God and others that you are truly great.

1. How do you define greatness? Name someone who you think is great and share your reason.
2. Do you think that God thinks that a drug dealer is great?
3. What could you do to be great?

CLOSING PRAYER

LIBERATION LESSON: TRIUMPHING THROUGH TEMPTATION

OPENING PRAYER

The bible states, "No temptation has seized you except what is common to man. And God is faithful; He will not let you be tempted beyond what you can bear. But when you are tempted, he will also provide a way out so that you can stand up under it."(I. Corinthian 10:13, 14) We are all tempted by something, some experience, some activity, some feeling or somebody. Show me a person who is not tempted and I will show you someone who no longer lives. Every red blooded human being knows what it is like to struggle with sin. Even Apostle Paul, missionary, church builder and writer of three-fourths of the New Testament confessed, "The good that I would do, that I do not. And the evil that I would not do, that I do...." (Romans 7) We all struggle with sin. We all make mistakes. We all have weaknesses. But our God provides a way out through His son Jesus Christ. Christ gives us grace, forgiveness, healing and liberation from our sins. It is through Him and with Him that we can triumph over our temptations. The victory is not in your own strength but in the strength and grace of God. When you are tempted, turn to Jesus Christ.

1. What are your temptations? (Weed, sex, wine, crack, money, material possessions, alcohol, etc.)
2. How do you feel after you fall from temptation?
3. When temptation comes at us, what does God want us to do?
4. How do you think prayer helps when you are tempted?

CLOSING PRAYER

LIBERATION LESSON: WINNERS AND LOSERS

OPENING PRAYER

Are you a winner or a loser? Many will say that they are winners because of their many possessions. They will brag about their $200 sneakers, trend setting clothes, expensive cars, their gaudy jewelry or roll of hundred dollar bills. There are those that say they are winners because they have a lot of women. They boast of their sexual conquest and even the children they created. There are those who say they are winners because of their arrogance and overly aggressive behavior. The world says only those who rule over others are winners, are victorious. But the bible tell us who the real winners are, "For everyone born of God overcomes the world, even our faith. Who is it that overcomes the world? Only he who believes that Jesus is the Son of God" (I. John 5:4, 5) The real winners, the real overcomers are those who have faith in our Lord and Savior Jesus Christ.

1. Are you a winner or a loser? Why?
2. What makes you a winner?
3. In what ways have you acted like a loser?
4. What kind of faith do you need to overcome the world?
5. What does it mean to overcome the world? Who is it that overcomes the world?

CLOSING PRAYER

LIBERATION LESSON: WHO IS YOUR SLAVE MASTER?

OPENING PRAYER

The bible states, "Therefore do not let sin reign in your mortal body so that you obey its evil desires. Do not offer the parts of your body to sin, as instruments of wickedness, but rather offer yourselves to God , as those who have been brought from death to life; and offer the parts of your body to him as instruments of righteousness. For sin shall not be your master, because you are not under law but under grace." (Romans 6:12-14)

1. What sin is your slave master? (sex , drugs, alcohol , violence, hatred , anger, greed)
2. What evil desires do you obey?
3. You must make a daily choice to either offer your body to sin or to God. What will you do today and why?
4. What can you do daily to make Jesus your master or Lord?

CLOSING PRAYER

LIBERATION LESSON: FREE FROM SIN

OPENING PRAYER

MEDITATION

The bible shares, Jesus replied, "I tell you the truth, everyone who sins is a slave to sin. Now a slave has no permanent place in the family, but a son belongs to it forever. So if the Son sets you free, you will be free indeed." (John 8:34-36) There are many people who are slaves to their passions and lust. They are unable to break free for their bad habits. Only Jesus Christ can liberate us from our sins. He breaks the chains of our sin with His truth and grace. He tells us the harsh truth about ourselves and then offers grace to forgive and free us.

1. What is sin to you?
2. What are the sins or the bad things that you do?
3. What does it mean to be a slave to sin?
4. Jesus promised to set you free. Have you acknowledged that you are powerless to your sin and need Him to free you?
5. What areas of your life do you need to be set free?

CLOSING PRAYER

LIBERATION LESSON: WHO ARE YOU HANGING OUT WITH?

OPENING PRAYER

MEDITATION

Who are your peers? Who is in your crew? Who is your gang? Who are the people you hang out with and are they helping you or hurting you? Often we associate with friends who may be good to us but not good for us. They may make us feel wanted and appreciated but they do not help us to become better people? Do they bring out the best in us or the worst in us? Do they hinder us in our devotion to God and help us to be more faithful Christians? We must be very careful who we spend quality time with. They will inevitably change our character, develop our perceptions, guide our behavior and shape our souls. That is why the bible states, "Do not be yoked together with unbelievers. For what do righteousness and wickedness have in common? Or what fellowship can light have with darkness? What harmony is there between Christ and Beliel? What does believer have in common with an unbeliever?" (II.Corinthians 6:14-7:1) You should spend more time with Christian believers and those who can bring out the best in you.

1. Who are your close friends and why?
2. Do they encourage you in your faith? Why or why not?
3. Why is it bad to hang out with unbelievers?
4. Why is it good to hang out with believers?
5. Why are gangs bad for young people?
6. What would happen if you left your gang, peers or unbelievers?

CLOSING PRAYER

LIBERATION LESSON: FORGIVEN AND CLEANSED OF SINS

OPENING PRAYER

The bible states, "If we claim to be without sin, we deceive ourselves and truth is not in us. If we confess our sins, he is faithful and just and will forgive our sins and cleanse us of all unrighteousness. If we claim we have not sinned, we make him out to be a liar and his word has no place in our lives."(I. John 1:8-`10) We all sin. We all make mistakes. We are have failed in something. Nobody is perfect. Therefore we need to confess your sins, mistakes, faults and failures to God. Tell God what you did wrong and He will forgive you. There is nothing that you can't say or do that God won't forgive. Confess your sins, He will forgive and heal your soul.

1. What are your sins?
2. Have you confessed your sins to God?
3. Why is it good to confess your sin to God?
4. Why is it bad not to confess your sins to God?
5. What does it mean to be cleansed of all unrighteousness?
6. Jesus is faithful and just to forgive you and cleanse you? Why is this good?

CLOSING PRAYER

LIBERATION LESSON: YOU CAN'T FALTER, SLIP OR SLEEP

OPENING PRAYER

MEDITATION

How is it that a shy, fatherless African American adolescent drug dealer can rise to become a multi-millionaire media mogul, hip hop entrepreneur and philanthropist? How is it that a thug who associated with drug dealers, substance abusers, and social deviants become a confidant of the President of the United States and a good will ambassador to Africa? How did Shawn Corey Carter aka Jay Z survive the mean streets of Brooklyn's drug-infested Marcey project and become the prosperous, powerful man he is today? Jay Z tells us, "You can want success all you want. But to get it. You can't falter. You can't slip. You can't sleep. One eye open, for real, forever." For Jay Z success did not come easy. Nobody gave it to him. He did not just dream and fantasize about it. He had to work hard and do everything he could to make it. He had to struggle and sacrifice to get what he wanted. Jay Z knew what it was to be born in the ghetto but he refused to stay in the ghetto. He knew the sting of rejection but he would not let it stop him. He knew what it was to survive in a drug infested community but he would not let the chains hold him back. His dreams, his vision was greater than his social economic environment. If Jay Z could do it then so can you. There is no reason in the world that you cannot break your chains and become prosperous and powerful. But you must be willing to pay the price for success. Remember" you can't falter, you can't slip and you can't sleep" and you can have whatever your want.

1. What do you think about Jay Z?
2. What are your dreams or vision of success?
3. What does it mean not to slip?
4. What does it mean not to falter?
5. What does it mean not to sleep?

CLOSING PRAYER

Chapter Six

Transforming Trouble Makers Into Peacemakers

"Blessed are the peace makers for they shall be called the children of God."(Matthew 5:9)

Our great, grand and glorious God is able to transform troublemakers into peacemakers. God is able to change drug dealers, substance abusers, gangsters and criminals into saved, sanctified Saints of God. There is no one that God cannot redeem, revive, reform and renew to his glory. Our God has liberated crack addicts, heroin addicts, pimps, prostitutes and player haters. He has set free alcoholics, rapist, cocaine addicts, thugs, homosexuals, sexual addicts, car jackers and gangsters. It matters not how baneful the behavior, corrupt the character, perverted the perspective and enslaved the soul. God is able to change anybody, anytime and anyplace. Look at the biblical record. It is God who took a hotheaded, murderer like Moses made him a great Liberator and a lawmaker. It was God who transformed a prostitute named Mary Magdalene and made her the first to proclaim his resurrection. God used a drunk like Noah to repopulate the earth and reestablish his dominion. King David committed adultery with Bathsheba, murdered Uriah, yet God still used him. Jonah was a bigot who refused to preach to the Ninevites and yet God still did a great work. Abraham was so cowardly that he would not acknowledge his wife before strangers, yet God made him the Father of all nations. Impetuous Peter abandoned our Lord, yet God established the church on his faith.

Saul persecuted and murdered the early Christians, but God changed his name to Paul and established churches in His name. Personally, I am a living witness of the gargantuan grace of God. If God can take a whore mongering, disco dancing, d-grade level, low life and save his soul, send him to Harvard Divinity School, make him a pastor and write a book through him, He can do anything! There is nobody that God cannot save and change. The Bible is right," If any man be in Christ, he is a new creature, old things pass away, behold all things become new." (II. Corinthians 5:17) It doesn't matter what these young boys have done in the past, God can forgive them and give them a bright future. They may have been poor students and dropped out school. Our God can take the worlds drop outs and make them biblical scholars of the Word of God. They may have been angry, hostile bullies, disrespecting their elders, threatening and intimidating people. But once they allow God in their life, they will become strong, sensitive and loving men of God. Our God is able to transform troublemakers into peacemakers. Our African American adolescent males can learn to be peace loving, God fearing children of God. They can be at peace with their family, peers and the world.

I have seen God do miracles with young African American males. God is the answer to the plethora of problems and pathologies that plague young African American males. The gospel of Jesus Christ is the spiritual solution to the problems of African American young man. They need to know about the death, burial and resurrection of Jesus Christ. They need to realize that Jesus suffered on the cross for their sins and was buried and on the third day rose from the grave. They need to understand that," God so loved the world that he gave his only begotten son so that whosoever believe in him, should not perish, but have everlasting life." (John 3:16) They need to know that the only way they could have peace in this life and in the next life is having a personal relationship with the Prince of Peace Jesus Christ. Once they have accepted Jesus Christ as their Lord and Savior then they can become peacemakers. Jesus said, "Blessed are the peacemakers for they shall be children of God." (Matthew 5:9) A peacemaker is someone who is at peace with themselves with God and with others. Moreover they pursue peace in the world.

In this chapter the laity will learn how to introduce Jesus Christ as Lord and Savior to the youth. They will teach them about the Prince of peace Jesus Christ and how he lived nonviolently and courageously with others. The youth will learn all the characteristics that make one a peacemaker. Finally they will be taught Christian Conflict Resolution classes that will deal with a wide variety of subjects such as anger management, nature of conflict, win-win scenarios, forgiveness, peacemaking process and making peaceful resolution with others.

HOW TO MAKE PEACEMAKERS

The gospel of Jesus Christ is the key to the liberation process of young, African American males. Once they have repented of their sins and accepted Jesus Christ as their Lord and Savior the shackles begin to drop off. Slowly but surely the psychological, spiritual and social chains fall and they experience freedom. The laity must instruct the youth in the transformation process from being troublemakers into peacemakers.

1. The youth must acknowledge the fact that "all have sinned and fallen short of the glory of God." Young men must accept that they have sinned against God and must repent of their sins.
2. The young boys need to know that Jesus Christ took their punishment upon the cross. Jesus suffered, bled and died on the cross. The bible says, "He was wounded for our transgressions. He was bruised for our iniquities." (Isaiah 53:5)
3. The boys need to understand that Jesus died on the cross and was buried. He laid dead on Friday and Saturday.
4. The boys should realize that early Sunday morning Jesus Christ rose from the grave and sits at the right hand of the father as King of Kings and Lord of Lord.
5. Finally the boys must, "confess with their mouth the Lord Jesus and believe in their heart that God raised him from the dead, they will be saved."(Romans 10:9,10)

Once they understand the biblical principles of salvation in Christ they can be led in the sinner's prayer to salvation. Let them recite this prayer,

"ALL MIGHTY GOD, I REPENT OF ALL OF MY SINS. I BELIEVE JESUS WAS CRUCUFIED ON THE CROSS FOR MY SINS WAS DEAD AND BURIED AND ROSE FROM THE GRAVE. I ACCEPT YOU JESUS CHRIST AS MY LORD AND SAVIOR. I ACCEPT YOU INTO MY HEART TODAY AND WILL LIVE FOR YOU FOREVER. AMEN "After the young man has recited this prayer, congratulate him and celebrate the victory with him. Encourage him to constantly pray, read his bible and regularly attend worship services. Since the boy knows the Prince of Peace he can now be trained to be a Peacemaker.

A Peacemaker has certain Christian characteristics that enable him to be at peace with his parent, siblings, his peers and the world. Peacemakers are peaceful, patient, prayerful, purposeful, passionate and positive. The laity will train the youth in all of these virtues and encourage them to apply them in their daily life.

PEACEMAKER TRAINING # 1

I. OPENING PRAYER

II. PEACEMAKERS ARE PEACEFUL

A PEACEMAKER MUST BE A PEACEFUL PERSON. THE SHOULD BE AT PEACE WITH THEMSELVES. GOD HAS GIVEN THEM AN INNER PEACE THAT CAN NOT BE DISTURBED BY ANYONE OR ANYTHING. READ THE FOLLOWING SCRIPTURES

1. I. Corinthians 1:10 Philippians 4:7; John 14:27
2. Luke 6:36; Matthew 5:7; James 2:12-13
3. James 1:19; II.Timothy 2:24-26

III. WHAT ARE SOME OF THE THINGS THAT DISTURB YOUR INNER PEACE?

1.
2.
3.

IV. WHAT CAN YOU DO OR SAY WHEN SOMEONE DISTURBS YOUR PEACE?

1. Ignore it - Proverbs 19:11
2. Bear it- Col.3:13, 15
3. Endure it- I.Peter 2:20, 23; 4:19
4. Forgive it- Matthew 6:14

V. DO A ROLE PLAY OF SOMEONE TRYING TO DISTURBING SOMEONES PEACE

1. What are some things that you could do?

2. Why is it important that you don't let anyone disturb your peace?
3. If someone can get you angry, who is really in control?
4. How does the Lord help you to keep your peace?

CLOSING PRAYER

PEACEMAKER TRAINING #2

I. OPENING PRAYER

II. PEACEMAKERS ARE PATIENT

A PEACEMAKER MUST BE PATIENT. PATIENTS IS A NECESSARY VIRTUE IF A YOUNG PERSON IS TRYING TO MAKE PEACE WITH OTHERS. DEVELOPING PEACE AND HARMONY CAN BE A PAINFUL, PROTRACTED PROCESS. IT MAY MEAN GETTING CALLED ALL KINDS OF NAMES, REJECTED, PERSECUTED, VILIFIED AND OSTRACIZED. INSPITE OF ALL THE INSULTS THE PEACEMAKER MUST BE PATIENT AND FORGIVING. THEY MUST OVERCOME EVIL WITH GOOD. READ THE FOLLOWING SCRIPTURES:

1. PATIENCE- James 5:7-8
2. FORGIVING-Mark 11:25
3. ENDURING-James 1:2-4

III. ARE YOU WILLING TO BE PATIENT AND FORGIVING? WHY OR WHY NOT?

1.
2.
3.

IV. IN WHAT WAYS IS JESUS PATIENT AND FORGIVING TO YOU?

1.
2.
3.

V. HOW CAN YOU BE PATIENT AND FORGIVING TO OTHERS?

CLOSING PRAYER

PEACEMAKER TRAINING #3

I. OPENING PRAYER

II. PEACEMAKERS ARE PRAYERFUL

THE ONLY WAY YOU CAN BE A PEACEMAKER IS THAT YOU "PRAY WITHOUT CEASING". THE PEACEMAKER MUST CONSTANTLY SEEK THE WISDOM, GUIDANCE AND THE ANOINTING OF GOD. THE ONLY WAY THAT YOU CAN DEAL WITH CONFLICT AND AGGRESSIVE PEOPLE IS BY PRAYER. PRAYER IS SIMPLY TALKING TO GOD.

III. READ THE FOLLOWING SCRIPTURES ON PRAYER

1. Matthew 7:7-8
2. Matthew 6:6
3. Isaiah 58:9
4. Mark 11:24

IV. HOW CAN PRAYER HELP YOU WHEN YOU DEAL WITH DIFFICULT PEOPLE?

V. WHAT KIND OF PRAYER SHOULD YOU HAVE WHEN YOU'RE IN CONFLICT?

VI. IN THE MIDST OF CONFLICT YOUR PRAYER MUST BE TO GIVE GOD GLORY

CLOSING PRAYER

PEACEMAKING TRAINING #4

I.   OPENING PRAYER

II. PEACEMAKER IS PURPOSEFUL

A PEACEMAKER UNDERSTANDS THAT HIS PRIMARY PURPOSE IN LIFE IS TO GLORIFY GOD. THEREFORE THE PEACEMAKER MUST GIVE GOD PRAISE AND GLORY EVEN IN THE MIDST OF CONFLICT. MOREOVER THE PEACEMAKER IS NOT INTERESTED IN WINNING THE ARGUMENT BUT MAKING SURE THAT GOD IS GLORIFIED IN THE PROCESS.

III. READ THE FOLLOWING SCRIPTURES ABOUT PRAISING AND GLORIFYING GOD

1. John 4:24; Psalm 95:6, 7
2. Psalm 100
3. Psalm 34

IV. IF YOU LOSE YOUR COOL WHILE YOU ARE IN CONFLICT, YOU NOT GIVING GOD GLORY. WHY?

V. HOW CAN YOU GIVE GOD GLORY WHEN YOU'RE IN CONFLICT WITH SOMEONE?

CLOSING PRAYER

PEACEMAKER TRAINING #5

OPENING PRAYER

I. PEACEMAKER IS PASSIONATE PERSON OR THEY ARE A LOVING PERSON. PEACEMAKER MUST BE MOTIVATED BY THE LOVE OF GOD. WHAT EVER THEY SAY AND DO IS OUT OF LOVE. THEREFORE IF THEY ARE IN CONFLICT WITH SOMEONE THEY MUST SHOW THEM LOVE. GOD LOVES US WE OUGHT TO LOVE ONE ANOTHER.

II. READ THE FOLLOWING SCRIPTURES ON LOVE

1. I. Corinthians 13
2. John 13:34, 35
3. I. John 3:18

III. HOW CAN YOU BE LOVING TO SOMEONE YOU ARE IN CONFLICT WITH?

IV. WHY WOULD JESUS TELL US TO LOVE OUR ENEMIES? READ MATTHEW 5:38-48

V. HOW DOES GOD GIVE YOU STRENGTH TO LOVE YOUR ENEMIES?

CLOSING PRAYER

PEACEMAKER TRAINING #6

OPENING PRAYER

I. PEACEMAKER IS POSITIVE OR SOMEONE WHO BELIEVES IN THE IMPOSSIBLE. THE PEACEMAKER "WALKS BY FAITH NOT BY SIGHT." THEY HAVE FAITH THAT JESUS CHRIST WALKS AND TALKS WITH THEM. THEY HAVE FAITH IN JESUS, THEMSELVES AND THE PEACEMAKING PROCESS. IT TAKES FAITH TO DEAL WITH DIFFICULT PEOPLE AND BELIEVE THAT GOD CAN CREATE PEACE AND HARMONY.

II. READ THE FOLLOWING SCRIPTURES ON FAITH

1. Hebrews 11:1-6
2. Mark 11:22-23
3. John 20:29

III. HOW CAN HAVING FAITH IN GOD HELP YOU WHEN YOU ARE IN CONFLICT?

VI. HOW CAN HAVING FAITH IN YOURSELF HELP YOU MAKE PEACE WITH OTHERS?

CLOSING PRAYER

CHRISTIAN CONFLICT RESOLUTION CLASS

"Bless those who curse you, do good to those who despitefully use you." Matthew 5:44

Some African American males are desperately in need of Christian Conflict Resolution Class. There are so many overly aggressive, angry, violent young males hurting and killing each other. The hostility and self-hatred among young African American males is slowly but surely destroying lives. Every day in some ghetto a young Black male is killing another Black male. Every day there is a drive-by shooting killing an innocent little child. Every day there is gang-related violence. Every day some mother is crying because her son has been killed. The Black on Black violence has to stop. We must end the bloodshed. We must end the mayhem and the madness. Enough is enough.

How do we end the violence? First of all the government can't stop the gun violence. They can improve the gun laws but they can't stop someone from killing someone. If there was a police officer on every street corner, they could not stop someone from getting a gun, knife or a bat and murdering someone. Stopping the sale of guns and assault rifles will help to end some of the bloodshed. But the only one who can penetrate the hostile human heart and infuse it with love, grace and peace is Jesus Christ. Only the Prince of Peace, Jesus Christ can give us inner peace that we may have peace with others. Jesus Christ can give young Black males peace, teach them Christian Conflict Resolution Skills and end the senseless violence in the neighborhood. The ultimate answer to the problem of guns and violence in the Black community is Jesus Christ and his principles of nonviolence. Christian Conflict Resolution Classes offered by the Church can end the hemorrhaging in the community.

I respectfully acknowledge that some of the information in the Christian Conflict Resolution Classes are based on the time proven classes used with such success in the great program of The PALS Conflict Resolution Program. The major modifications are its Christological and biblical emphasis. Also, I am especially grateful for the insights and information by our own conflict resolution expert Rev. Peek Vary.

Christian Conflict Resolution differs from other conflict resolution paradigms. Christian Conflict Resolution emphasizes the Prince of Peace Jesus Christ as our ultimate role model of a nonviolent life style. Moreover Christian Conflict Resolution uses biblical principles and scriptures to inform and inspire young people to find healthy harmonious ways to resolve their conflict. The Prince of Peace once taught, "Blessed are the peacemakers they shall become the children of God."(Matthew 5:9) He also taught," You have heard that has been said an eye for an eye and a tooth for tooth, but I say unto you that ye resist not evil but whosoever shall smite thee on the right cheek, turn to him the other. … You have heard that it has been said, you shall love thy neighbor and hate thine enemy. But I say unto you love your enemies, bless them that curse you, do good to them that hate you, and pray for those that despitefully use you and persecute you, that you may be children of your Father which is in Heaven, for He makes his sun to rise on the evil and on the good and sets the rain on the just and the unjust."(Matthew 5:38-45) Jesus not only taught nonviolence, he lived it. In spite of the constant criticism, name calling, mocking, ridicule and threats to his life he remained nonviolent. Hate crucified Him, but love resurrected Him. The malice of men murdered Him, but the mercy of God raised Him. They beat and bruised His body, but they could not break His spirit. Jesus' love triumphed over the world's wickedness. He showed us how to live nonviolently with love, forgiveness, faith, peace and hope. These Christian principles are the foundation of Christian Conflict Resolution Classes.

Christian Conflict Resolution Classes will train the boys to have an argument with someone without resorting to guns and violence. They will learn how to create a peaceful resolution. Christian Conflict Resolution is identifying and implementing Christian solutions to the conflict or argument. The best answers are those that are nonviolent, meet the needs of the people involved, improve relationships of those people and give glory to God. Christian Conflict Resolution will prepare young African

American males to acquire Christian characteristic to cope with divisive issues in a nonviolent manner.

TENTANTS OF CHRISTIAN CONFLICT RESOLUTION

The tenants of Christian Conflict Resolution are found in the Holy Scriptures and in the nonviolent life of the Prince of Peace Jesus Christ. This will be a fundamental challenge to our young people. They may reject it at first. It goes against their life style. Consequently, they will have to repent of their bullying behavior, anger and hostility. They will have to learn the principles of nonviolence, forgiveness and rediscover other points of view to reach mutually satisfying agreements. If we can succeed in teaching our young men this framework for resolving their disputes the results for them and our community will be miraculous. Christian Conflict Resolution will provide the skills and processes for them to manage and resolve conflict constructively. When they experience successful conflict resolution there will be more likely to use the Christian conflict resolution process elsewhere in their lives. Christian Conflict Resolution provides our youth with the biblical knowledge, abilities and processes needed to end their self-destructive lifestyle. Young men need to be challenged to live the Christian life of love, faith, hope and forgiveness.

It is the moral responsibility of the church to teach Christian Conflict Resolution Classes. This will enable African American youth to become more respectful, responsible, resilient and reverent. They will become more cooperative in their homes. There will be less sibling rivalry and more respect given to the parents. The youth will learn the ability to share, how to listen and there will be greater family harmony. Some of the blessings of these classes is that the youth will become more empowered to take responsibility for their feelings and their actions. They will cultivate a positive self-esteem and develop their decision-making skills. They will gain peer respect and recognition and will learn how to decide their own fate. Finally they will get a closer walk with our Lord and Savior Jesus Christ. They will become Peacemakers in their homes, schools and community. The more the adolescent African American males attend the

Christian Conflict Resolution classes the greater peace they will have within themselves, amongst their peers and in our community.

CHRISTIAN CONFLICT RESOLUTION

OVERVIEW

1. PEACEMAKER PLEDGE
2. NATURE OF CONFLICT
3. ELEMENTS OF CONFLICT
4. CONFLICT AND VIOLENCE
5. DIFFERENCES IN CONFLICT RESOLUTION APPROACHES
6. TWO APPROACHES TO CONFLICT
7. WIN/WIN AND WIN/LOSE
8. THREE-LEVELS OF CONFLICT
9. STYLES OF HANDLING CONFLICT
10. PEACEMAKERS WAY TO HANDLE CONFLICT
11. ANGER MANAGEMEMENT
12. PEACEMAKER PROCESS

PEACEMAKER PLEDGE

1. I PLEDGE MY LOYALTY TO JESUS CHRIST AS LORD, SAVIOR AND PRINCE OF PEACE.
2. I PLEDGE TO BE A PEACEMAKER BY BEING NONVIOLENT, LOVING, FORGIVING, PATIENT, PEACEFUL, PRAYERFUL AND POSITIVE.
3. I PLEDGE TO UNDERSTAND CONFLICT AND SEE TO ITS PEACEFUL, HARMONIOUS RESOLUTION.
4. I PLEDGE TO BE EMPATHETIC AND RESPECTFULL OF THE FEELINGS, PERCEPTIONS AND IDEAS OF OTHERS.
5. I PLEDGE TO NOT BE MOTIVATED BY MY ANGER OR FEELINGS BUT BY MY FAITH AND LOVE OF GOD.
6. I PLEDGE TO PURSUE A PEACEFUL PROCESS TO ENSURE THAT THE PRINCE OF PEACE IS GLORIFIED.

7. I PLEDGE TO BE AN EFFECTIVE COMMUNICATOR BY LISTENING AND UNDERSTANDING ALL THOSE PERSONS WHO ARE IN CONFLICT.

8. I PLEDGE TO BE LED BY THE HOLY SPIRIT IN HOW I RELATE AND COMMUNICATE WITH THOSE IN CONFLICT.

9. I PLEDGE TO PRAY FOR THOSE I AM IN CONFLICT AND ALWAYS FORGIVE THEM.

10. I PLEDGE TO SET AN EXAMPLE AND TEACH OTHERS HOW TO BE A PEACEMAKER.

NATURE OF CONFLICT

We should understand the nature of conflict and teach it to young African American males. They must realize that everyone has conflicts. Conflict is natural. It is a part of our everyday lives. Even though we can learn to deal with conflict, it will continue to exist. Conflict is sometimes a necessary part of life. Conflict exist on all levels of all relationships, from the interpersonal to the international. The spiritual root of all conflict is sin. (James 4:1-3) Conflict is caused by differences in perception. We all see the world differently based on our experiences, needs, feelings, culture, family background and values. Conflict allows us to grow and learn. Conflict itself does not destroy relationships. It is the unwillingness to handle conflicts that ruins relationships. Conflict has many causes like a lack of understandings, power and control. People handle conflicts in different ways. Words, actions and body language can trigger a conflict. Our values greatly influence our behavior and the decision we make. Our values may cause conflict with others or within ourselves. Crises arises from a different needs, drives, wishes and, or demands. Conflict in and of itself is not positive or negative. Rather it is a response to conflict that transforms it into either a competitive, destructive experience or a constructive challenge offering the opportunity for growth. Since conflict is an inevitable part of life, learning how to respond to it constructively is essential. Conflict resolution begins with developing an understanding of conflict in the principles of conflict resolution. Conflict is a condition of opposition wherein there is a clash of interests. One party's actions adversely affect another's. Two or more parties have an unresolved controversy. Again the cause of conflict are different perceptions, goals, expectations, misunderstandings, resources time, money, position, space, goods, property, values, and unmet needs. Conflict is a dynamic process and it initiates change through growth or destruction. Conflict itself does not destroy relationships. The inability or unwillingness to handle conflict destroys relationships. One's perceptions, thoughts, values and feelings dictate the meaning of conflict situations, and strongly shape their outcomes. Conflict is productive when it attacks problems not people. The collective effect of many minor problems are conflicts that are not resolved constructively have a detrimental effect on the whole system. To enable young African American males to understand the conflicts that they may be dealing with the following questions are asked:

1. How do you react when you are angry, frustrated or hurt?
2. What do you do when you have a conflict with someone?
3. Why do people argue and fight?
4. What are some ineffective ways to handle conflict?
5. Develop a list of the things that young boys fight about.
6. Develop a list of the things that adults fight about.
7. Develop a list of things that world leaders fight about.
8. What does the Bible says about conflict, wars and fight? Read James 4:1-7

THE ELEMENTS OF CONFLICT

Every conflict involves three basic elements: the issue, the relationship and the emotions. If we consider this information, rather than act merely on our impulse, we increase the likelihood of creating positive change.

I. THE ISSUE

The things that caused the conflict and that need to be addressed in order to resolve the conflict

II.   THE RELATIONSHIP

The association or connection between the youths. The nature of the relationship affects the youth's perceptions of the issue and dynamics of the conflict.

III.   THE EMOTIONS

How the youth feel. The emotions may be related to, but not the same as, the issue.

VI.   THE CHALLENGE

When you are in conflict, analyze the situation before you act. Ask yourself:

1.   What is my issue?
2.   What is my relationship with the other person?
3.   How am I feeling?
4.   What can I do to give God glory in this conflict?

CONFLICT AND VIOLENCE

"He that lives by the sword, will perish by the sword."
Matthew 26:52

Young African American males need to understand the myths and the nature of violence. We all have the right to feel safe and to be safe. Violence violates this right. The scars of violence impact every generation. Exposure to violence hinders the development of self-esteem, the capacity to trust, the ability to feel happy, safe and loved and the skills to learn. It distorts perceptions of others, and detains social and spiritual growth. Victims of violence may be prone to emotional isolation, uncontrolled anger and inadequate behavior. They're likely to have an incapacity for empathy, intimacy and fulfilling relationships. The consequences and costs of violence in our society are enormous for all of us. Young victims are less likely to become peaceful citizens and continue the cycle of violent behavior as perpetrators themselves.

WHAT IS VIOLENCE?

Violence is any use of power which causes people pain, harm, or in any way violates their dignity. It could be force used to injure or take advantage of someone. This may be through physical, verbal, psychological, and or institutional means. Violence is a willful disregard for another with a direct or indirect harm. Violence is beyond physical hurting, it is the deprivation of any basic human need. The Hebrew word most often translated as violence is "Chama" or unjust gain, cruelty, damage, injustice by an oppressor, unrighteousness, and wrong. One Greek word translated to mean violence, intimidation or force is "Osseo".

The contributing factors to violence are exposure to violence, retaliation, the lack of human rights, intense anger, racism, sexism, poverty, unemployment, and access to guns. Other contributing factors to violence are alcohol and other drug abuse. The media's glorification of violence. The perception of violence as manly or macho contributes to violence. There is a social permission or encouragement to use violence. Also the feeling of being belittled or put down, ridiculed, or receiving racial or ethnic slurs creates violence. We must understand that violence leads to more violence. Poverty, lack of job opportunities, and discrimination are strongly related to the propensity to use violence. Violent behavior is learned and can be unlearned. Violence is preventable.

THE MYTHS OF VIOLENCE

There are myths, attitudes and beliefs that reinforce violent behavior in our society. Many common, relatively mild forms of violent behavior often excused as normal, even unavoidable, passages of childhood. Often, for example, adults overlook or fail to criticize bullying, fighting, intimidation, harassment and name-calling. People often do not speak up when they hear about extreme forms of punishment or discipline meted out in the privacy of home or classroom. It is more common for adults to excuse explosive uncontrolled anger as normal expressions of emotion. They must appropriately take thoughtful steps to intervene and correct these patterns. To reduce the violence in our society we must question the social myths that are perpetuated.

MYTH # 1: VIOLENCE WORKS

Our youth are inundated with images of violence, murder and death. T.V, video games and rap music glorify violence, mobsters, hoodlums, renegade cops and desensitize our youth about violence. Our youth begin to believe violence is an acceptable and effective way to deal with conflict.

MYTH # 2: VIOLENT ACTS GO UNPUNISHED

Many of our youth are aware of perpetrators of violent acts still roam the streets. They have not been caught by the police and no one is snitching. This creates the illusion that those who use violence will get away with it.

MYTH # 3: VICTIMS BRING TROUBLE ON THEMSELVES

There is a belief that those who are victims of violence somehow got what was coming to them. There are those who believe that those who have been killed are finally getting what they deserve.

MYTH # 4: REAL MEN FIGHT AND USE VIOLENCE

Many African American males believe that they must act macho and fight. They will fight to be respected and receive esteem from other. They think that they should dominate women and weak boys. There is this notion that real men cannot be successful unless they always win and are on top.

In order to control violence we must discuss and debunk these myths on violence. Once our young people can acknowledge their attitudes and feelings about violence they will be able to engage in Christian Conflict Resolution. The following questions should be asked and discussed:

1. Has violence ever worked for you? Explain
2. Is it an accepted way to do things? Explain
3. Have you ever bullied someone? Explain
4. Have you ever been bullied? Explain
5. What is your attitude toward violence?
6. What are some of the subtle forms of violence within our society? (poverty, lack of medical care)
7. What are some of the subtle or overt forms of violence in the school?

DIFFERENCES IN CONFLICT RESOLUTION APPROACHES

TROUBLEMAKER APPROACH	PEACEMAKER APPROACH
Win – Lose resolution	Win-win resolution
Focus on own needs/wants	Focus on mutual needs
Closed communication	Open Communication
Narrow focus	expanded focus
Based on positions	Based on interest
Competitive	Collaborative
Self-centered	Christ-centered
Led by the flesh	Led by the Holy Spirit
Self-glorification	Glorification of God
Vindictive	Forgiving

TWO APPROACHES TO CONFLICT

There are two types of approaches to conflict they are: a win/win approach or a win/ lose approach. In the win/win approach the behaviors are problem-solving, respect, listening, forgiving, praying, and being led by the Holy Spirit. In the win/ lose the behaviors are disrespect, name-calling, not listening, and being led by the flesh.

In disputes, people usually believe that they know the right answer. They believe that their viewpoint should prevail. They believe that the only way to get what they want is to make sure that the other person does not get what he or she wants. In seeking a win/ win solution we need to invent creative broad options rather than looking for single narrow answers. We need to search for mutual gains and finally find ways to make decisions easy.

The Troublemaker, Adversarial conflict resolution or win/ lose is destructive to interpersonal relationships. When conflict is approached in an adversarial manner the mindset is a win/ lose mindset. This is in fact the way most people negotiate. This type of negotiation is like a contest where one person wins or gets what it is he or she wants and the other person loses and does not get what he or she wants. This kind of negotiation is also called positional-based negotiation as the focus is on what the person wants. In the positional-based negotiation negotiators build on the emotions. They get attached to their positions.

The Peacemaker or Non-adversarial conflict resolution has the potential to enhance interpersonal relationships. It is called win-win solution. A Win-win solution is interest-based and negotiation brings us closer to the resolution of conflict. In interest-based negotiation, we move away from what the person wants to why they want it, i.e. of what interest is it to them. It is when both people get some of what they want or need in a given situation. It is the win/win type of resolution we want to emphasize. We want our young boys to approach conflict from a win-win perspective and achieve win-win solutions.

When in conflict, people often use behaviors that they think will help them win, but as a result, the other person feels upset and does not like the outcome. By default, the other person becomes the loser. Whether we use the Peacemaker constructive win-win or the Troublemaker destructive win/lose methods to resolve a conflict depends, on if we believe that we can both be winners. The young boys must develop the Christian characteristics and skills and attitudes necessary for win-win. A win-win solution is specific and everyone understands the what, how, when and where necessary to resolve the conflict. In a win-win everyone involved in the conflict shares in the responsibility to solve it. In a win-win the plan for resolving the conflict is mutually satisfying and realistic. Finally in a win-win the feelings of everyone involved in the conflict are respected and heard. In a win/win God is glorified. Our young African American males need to be taught how to handle conflict from a Peacemakers win-win perspective. The following questions need to be asked of them:

1. Think of a conflict that ended in a win/win resolution. What allowed that to happen?
2. Think of conflict that ended in a win/lose resolution. What could you have done to have the outcome to be a win/win resolution?
3. Read Mark 10:35-45
    a. What was the conflict?
    b. What was James and Johns solution?
    c. What was Jesus solution to the conflict?
    d. If you were James and John what would you have done?
    e. If you were Jesus what would you have done?
    f. Was Jesus solution a win/win or win/lose? Why?

THREE LEVELS OF CONFLICT

There are three levels of conflict. The three levels of conflict are blips, clashes, and crisis. The blips are minor annoyances that are just a part of everyday life. On their own, they pose no threat to the relationship. They may be rooted in habits, personal mannerisms, different expectations, or another source. At this level, one may use nonviolent conflict resolution skills successfully to prevent the conflict from escalating to a higher level. The blips sometimes accumulate and grow into clashes. Clashes occur when there are repeated arguments about the same issue. Or their increasing number of issues that create a clash. Sometimes feeling less cooperative toward another party is a clash. A clash can occur when there is a lack of trust and honesty and good will. When people remain angry for long period of time it creates a clash. Finally when people begin to privately begin to question the value of the relationship it is a clash. At this level, the youth need to employ anger management skills to relieve the tension. A constructive problem-solving approach may still resolve the situation. The final level of conflict is called crisis. A crisis calls for additional intervention. Conflict that has risen to a crisis level may mean stress levels go up, eating disorders, abuse, or other compulsive behaviors. Another indicator of a crisis is the sense that relationships or situation is psychologically unhealthy. It means to be emotionally upset, use physical violence, vandalism, assault and battery, even murder. Once a crisis has been contained in the escalated, disputants may seek resolution and reconciliation but not until then. Intense confrontations, even after dispute is resolved, may require outside help. Adolescent African American males need to understand the three levels of conflict. Generate a discussion by asking the following questions:

1. WHAT IS A BLIP? GIVE AN EXAMPLE
2. HOW WOULD YOU HANDLE A BLIP?
3. WHAT IS A CLASH? GIVE AN EXAMPLE
4. HOW WOULD YOU HANDLE A CLASH?
5. WHAT IS A CRISES? GIVE AN EXAMPLE
6. HOW WOULD YOU HANDLE A CLASH?
7. HOW WOULD JESUS HANDLE A BLIP, CLASH, OR CRISES?

STYLES OF HANDLING CONFLICT

"My brethren count it all joy when you fall into various trials knowing that the testing of your faith produces patience." James 1:2

There are different styles of handling conflict. Each conflict management style has potential uses and potential limitations. We need to help our young boys recognize their style of handling conflict. They need to learn to judge the appropriateness of different styles to determine when and when not to use any particular one. They need to understand how the style they use affects our ability to resolve conflict. They need to identify assets and liabilities of each style. We have a choice in the conflict style we use and the one we use may depend on the issue and relationships involved in the conflict. The style of conflicts are Accommodating, Compromising, Avoiding, Competing, Collaborating, and Agreeing to Disagree. There are certain dynamics in each style of conflict and any of these approaches may be appropriate under certain circumstances. Our young boys need to know all the styles of handling conflict and know which one to use in an appropriate time.

ACCOMODATING STYLE OF HANDLING CONFLICT

In the Accommodating style of handling conflict, the main objective is to maintain the relationship at any cost .The way it is done is to conceal your needs, perceptions, or feelings. It means to agree and get along. The Accommodating style of conflict means you'll look away, speak softly, use plenty of qualifiers and surrender your beliefs and values so others will accept you. The Accommodating style of conflict says," love me and anything you want to do is fine with me." The advantages of the Accommodator is that it can preserve a relationship and it is good for the short term. It is also good when the relationship is more important than the issue. The disadvantages of this style is that it opens one up for being used. The other person is denied opportunity to grow and you risk being treated like a doormat. The other persons win is at your expense and you may never get your needs met.

COMPROMISING STYLE OF HANDLING CONFLICT

In the Compromising style of handling conflict the objective is a quick fix. The way it is done is to reveal your surface needs, but gloss over your underlying needs. Those who are compromising keep a direct eye contact and body orientation. They acknowledge others surface needs, perceptions and feelings. They use negotiation talk to get a quick solution, and a quick fix. They put results ahead of principles. The end justifies the means. The Compromiser says, "Let's make a deal and I've got an offer you can't refuse." The advantages of the Compromising style is that both persons have the same mindset and both are satisfied with the solution. It is useful when parties of equal strength have mutually exclusive goals and useful when all else fails. The disadvantages to this style is that an opportunity is missed for persons to benefit fully from the situation and it may avoid real issues in conflict.

AVOIDING STYLE OF HANDLING CONFLICT

In the Avoiding style of handling conflict the main objective is to minimize distress or discomfort. The way they do it is to conceal all their needs, perceptions and feelings. They look away, fidget, or just get up and leave. The Avoiding style of conflict turn their body away from others and focus on something else. They minimize or shun any discomfort, change the tone, or the subject. They resigned themselves to the situation as hopeless. The Avoiding style of conflict says," Nice day isn't it and there's nothing I can do." The disadvantage of the avoiding style is that the person is doesn't take responsibility for the situation. The Avoiding style of conflict is useful when confronting is too dangerous or damaging or when an issue is unimportant. It is also useful when a situation needs to" cool down" or when you want to buy time and prepare. The disadvantages of the Avoiding style is that important issues may never be addressed. Also the conflict may escalate or resurface later.

COMPETING STYLE OF HANDLING CONFLICT

In the Competing style of handling conflict the objective is winning is the only thing. The Competitor is only concerned with their desires. Their feelings are relevant and others are not. The Competitor uses messages, stereotypes, and labels, impugn, accuse and blame. They are rigid and polarize others. The Competitor style of conflict invades others' personal space. They get in close. They stare and glair. They intimidate people. They divide and conquer. They set their opponents against each other, and then clean up the spoils. The Competitor style of conflict says, "It's my way or no way." In the competitor style of conflict it facilitates a quick decision making which is sometimes necessary and useful when safety is a concern. It reveals leadership and it is useful when one believes one is right. Disadvantages of this style is that it does not allow others to participate and problem-solving. The other party feels disempowered and not respected.

COLLABORATING STYLE OF HANDLING CONFLICT

In the Collaborating style of conflict the main objective is to solve the problem by meeting as many needs as possible. The way this is done is by sharing appropriately any ideas or feelings that may help. They separate the person from the problem, treat all parties respectfully, regardless of their behavior. They identify underlining emotions rather focus on positions and building a team spirit. They listen attentively. They give constructive verbal feedback and listen to suggestions. They generate and point out options. They seek common ground. The Collaborator will say, "We are in the same boat. I feel upset about the problem but less work together to solve it." The advantages of the Collaborating style of conflict is that it allows for creative solutions, fosters good communication skills, meets interest, decision address everyone's needs, improves relations between people, and parties learn from each other's point of view. The disadvantages of the Collaborating style is that is time-consuming and will not work unless parties agree to the process.

AGREEING TO DISAGREE STYLE OF HANDLING CONFLICT

In the Agreeing to Disagree conflict style the main objective is to understand and respect others' behavior and values. In some conflicts, you may not want to use any of the above. You may disagree with someone about a complex social, political, moral or religious issue. Now with this view someone is willing to compromise their position, or values. They don't want to damage their personal or professional bond. They don't want to put the other party down or showing any sort of disrespect. They have accepted that there is an impasse. In this style they want to maintain the integrity of the relationship. Those who have an Agreeing to Disagree conflict style say," We can't agree on everything." Or they will say," we will never see eye to eye on this, but that's not going to interfere with how we are to get along."

Adolescent African American males need to be aware of their conflict style. They also need to be aware of the other conflict styles that are available to them to deal with every situation that confronts them. The following questions may be asked so that the boys can discover their conflict style and understand the other conflict styles available to them.

1. What do you think your style of handling conflict is and why?
2. Give an example of the time that you used a particular style of handling conflict?
3. What is the style of handling conflict that you do not like?
4. What is the style of handling conflict that is needed when someone wants to fight you?
5. What is the style of handling conflict that is needed when someone disrespects you?
6. What is the style of handling conflict when someone has a gun pointed at you?

PEACEMAKERS WAY TO HANDLE CONFLICT

1. PRAY AND TALK TO GOD ABOUT THE SITUATION AND THE PERSON. ASK GOD TO GIVE YOU THE RIGHT THOUGHTS, FEELINGS AND WORDS TO HANDLE THE CONFLICT.
2. LISTEN TO THE FEELINGS AND WORDS OF THE PERSON THAT YOU ARE IN CONFLICT WITH. TRY TO

SEE THINGS FROM THEIR PERSPECTIVE. EMPATHIZE WITH THEM.

3. IF THEY HAVE SAID OR DONE ANYTHING TO OFFEND YOU IMMEDIATELY FORGIVE THEM.

4. BE WILLING TO APOLOGIZE FOR YOUR PART IN THE CONFLICT. YOU MAY WANT TO SAY, "I AM SORRY WE ARE HAVING THIS PROBLEM."

5. BE WILLING TO COMPROMISE, NEGOTIATE AND FIND A COMMON GROUND SO THAT IT IS A WIN/WIN SOLUTION.

6. IF THERE IS A LOT OF EMOTIONS INVOLVED AND IT'S DIFFICULT TO DISCUSS THE CONFLICT AGREE TO TALK ABOUT IT LATER. WAIT UNTIL TEMPERS COOL DOWN.

7. IF IT IS STILL DIFFICULT TO COME TO AN AGREEMENT YOU MAY WANT TO ASK FOR AN OBJECTIVE MEDIATOR WHO YOU BOTH WANT. THEY CAN ASSIST IN WORKING WITH YOU TO DEVELOP A WIN/WIN SOLUTION.

8. ALWAYS REMEMBER THAT GOD HAS CALLED YOU TO BE A PEACEMAKER AND YOUR WEAPON IS LOVE. THE LOVE THAT GOD HAS GIVEN YOU IS UNCONDITONAL AND UNLIMITED. YOU MUST FORGIVE THE UNFORGIVEABLE, BEAR THE UNBEARABLE AND TOLERATE THE INTOLERABLE. THIS LOVE CAN TRANSFORM FOES INTO FRIENDS AND HOSTILITY INTO LOVE AND TRANQUILITY.

CHRISTIAN ANGER MANAGEMENT

"If you are angry, do not let it become sin, Get over your anger before the day is finished." Ephesians 4:26

Adolescent African American males need to control their anger so that they may use skills to preserve relationships, respect feelings and solve problems. They need to discuss anger as an emotion that has both positive and negative modes of expression. They need to recognize the different anger styles and demonstrate the value of formulating anger management plans. African-American males need to understand that anger is a natural emotion but it does not give them the license to hurt someone. They must learn to express emotions effectively and appropriately. Anger is a strong emotion and its intensity will affect the body, mind and heart. We all have power to take charge of our anger. It is important that African American males learn to work out their anger. They can learn to redirect it creatively and constructively. Making this switch can improve their interpersonal skills and correct injustices in our society and world. It is my hope that every African American male become aware of his anger and not go on the attack and hurt others. Unfortunately, many of them have come to believe that hurting others is okay. Also, many of them have never learned a more appropriate means of expressing anger. A lot of what they see in life and the media is a negative, destructive side of anger. If we take away their old attack plans we must replace them with the constructive behaviors. This is where our Christian anger management plan comes in.

It is important that African American males learn to cope with their anger. Often anger is used negatively, but we can learn to redirect it creatively and constructively. Making this switch can improve their interpersonal skills and give glory to God. Positive aspect of anger is that it is a signal. It alerts us that something is annoying, unjust, or threatening. Anger is an energizer. It can mobilize the body's resources for self-defense and provides us with stamina during difficult task. Therefore young African American males can channel their anger in positive ways. The negative aspects of anger is that we cannot think clearly or evaluate options rationally. We act more impulsively, without carefully considering the consequences of our behavior. When we feel hurt or embarrassed, anger makes us protect our pride. This sort of defensive anger prevents us from recognizing our feelings and facing ourselves honestly. Anger can evoke aggression. Sometimes adolescent African American males release their anger feelings by unleashing them on something or someone. Anger is a problem when it is too common, too intense, last too long, or disturbs work or relationships. African American males get angry when their goals or demands are blocked, their values are questioned, their life style is threatened and their rules are broken. The Bible warns us about the dangers of uncontrollable anger in Proverbs 29:22 & Matthew 5:22

Common sense tells us that the boys cannot always have, or do everything they want, when they want. When their wants or needs are blocked by other people or things, they feel frustrated. A frustrating experience can be a challenge that forces us to think creatively about how to solve a problem and become more capable people. When the young boys do not deal with their frustrations constructively, they begin to feel angry and desperate and may do things that hurt themselves and others. By helping African American males to increase their tolerance to frustration, we can decrease the likelihood of frustrating situations leading to anger or getting out of control.

There are ways to help African American males increase the tolerance to frustration. We need to help them determine if their frustration is caused by something they can change. We must continually point out the benefits of tolerating frustration. We must help them understand that nothing has to go their way because they want it to. We should verbally praise the boy's attempts to tolerate frustration and challenge them when they exhibit low frustration.

African American males need to know the triggers that unleash their anger. It is important for them to know how particular people, events, actions may affect their anger and behavior. They must understand that anger is an emotion that is normal. But uncontrollable anger causes people to fight, argue, take drugs, steal, vandalize and kill. Anger can cause people to make destructive or constructive changes. The following questions need to be answered so that the young males can understand the triggers that unleash their anger.

1. What are some of the things that people do that make you angry?
2. Do you have any painful experiences of anger that you would like to share?
3. Are you angry or frustrated about something right now?

4. What triggers your anger?
5. What is your physical response?
6. How do you usually deal with difficult situations that make you angry?
7. What are the results?
8. Is your approach effective for getting what you need or want?
9. What might you try to do differently?
10. Jesus helps us to control our anger and respond with love. Read Philippians 2:13 ; James 1:19,20 ; Proverb 19:11; Matthew 5:23-25 ; Proverbs 15:1,18 ; 21:14 ; Proverb 21:19

PEACEMAKER PROCESS

1. THE PEACEMAKER MUST ALWAYS GLORIFY GOD. WE SHOULD PLEASE GOD AT ALL TIMES. (I. Corinthians 10:31)
2. THE PEACEMAKER MUST ALWAYS EXAMINE HIMSELF. HE MUST CHECK HIS ATTITUDE, FEELINGS, FAULTS AND PERCEPTIONS. (Matthew 7:5)
3. THE PEACEMAKER MUST HAVE A CONSTRUCTIVE CONFRONTATION. THEY MUST BE WILLING TO TELL THE TRUTH WITH LOVE AND GRACE. (Matthew 18:15)
4. THE PEACEMAKER MUST BE WILLING TO DO WHATEVER IS NECESSARY TO RESTORE THE RELATIONSHIP. (Matthew 5:24)

Shade, Ken., The Peacemaker. pgs. 10, 11. Baker Book house, Grand Rapids, Michigan. 1977.

Chapter Seven

"Sing a song. If you sing a song a day, you will make a better day." Earth, Wind and Fire

Liberating Lyrics

One of the more powerful, influences in our society is music. Music is a universally appreciated medium that inspires people from all walks of life. Music has power to reach us on a very deep emotional and spiritual level. It can fill us with uncontrollable joy. It can bring tears to our eyes. It can make us feel sad and blue. Music has the power to make the weak feel strong and the strong feel weak. Music can motivate people to do good or to do evil. It can encourage people to be rebellious, promiscuous and hostile or it can inspire holiness, philanthropy and community service. Music can challenge us to stand up for our rights and fight for our freedoms. Or it can fill our minds with superfluous, non-essential information that makes us happy but dulls our social consciousness. Listening to music can be a therapeutic experience bringing healing to our souls. Music can be a time machine bringing back fond memories or taking you to the future with hopeful anticipation. Music can motivate us to worship God and live a godly lifestyle. On the other hand, music can instill vacuous values that make us ungodly, hedonistic and narcissistic. Some lyrics liberate the heart, mind and soul while other lyrics enslave us to the whims and caprices of the flesh.

The reason why music has such an influence on the human spirit is because of its spirituality. Country Western, Gospel, Spirituals, Classical, R@B, Hip Hop, Blues, Jazz, Rock @ Roll, Techno-Beat or Rap is spiritual because it stems from our heart and soul. Not all music is religious because they all do not refer to God, faith or the Bible. But all music is spiritual because it stems from the passion and perceptions of humanity. The spirituality of music is what touches the heart, mind and soul of an individual.

Rap music is no exception. Rap music is extremely popular among young African American males. Rap music is spiritual because it speaks to the values, feelings, hopes and dreams of millions. For many young African American males it validates their thoughts and passions. They listen to it religiously and find comfort and joy in it. Rap music speaks to the souls of some of our young people. It reflects who they are what they feel and what they are all about.

If the older generation wants to reach the next generation they must begin to understand rap music. Those of us past fifty years of age might not like rap music. We may detest the profanity, racial derogatory, misogynistic, materialistic, hedonistic, narcissistic lyrics of rap music. We may believe that it is responsible for the moral, psychological downfall of many young African Americans. We may denounce it or not listen to it but we cannot afford to ignore it. To ignore rap music is to ignore an essential aspect of our young people.

My teenage son enjoys listening to Rap music. He enjoys the rhythm, beat and some of the catchy lyrics of rap music. He listens to it constantly and has been inspired to create his own rap songs. Several times I put on his head sets , listened to his music and was completely disgusted. Some of his rap music I could not stand. But If I wanted to enhance our relationship I had to stop criticizing and condemning his music. I had to learn to listen beyond the profanity and hear the message. Once I stopped judging and started listening I found creative way to teach the gospel. We listened to his songs, discussed them and applied the gospel to them. My son and I had some interesting conversations .Interestingly, the more we discussed rap songs the more enlightened we became. I learned some things about my son and his ability to discern the positive and negative aspects of rap. He learned the negative values that the songs were espousing and what the bible has to say about it. Moreover, I discovered that if I listened beyond the profanity, there is a message that can liberate our youth. There are some rap songs whose lyrics can assist in their liberation process. My son and some of my young church members are a living witness of how our God can work through rap music and liberate the soul.

Liberating Lyrics are songs that can liberate the slave mentality of our youth. I have used Rap, Hip Hop, R@B, and Reggae music as a basis for brief meditations and reflective questions. The discussion leader, mentor, Sunday school teacher , parent or youth leader can down load the rap song, play it for the boys and challenge the corrupt values found in Rap music and share their inspirational message. The purpose of Liberating Lyrics is to raise the conscious level of the youth and liberate their spirits. This exercise will help our youth to know the truth and the truth will set them free.

There are those who would argue that these rap songs shouldn't even be mentioned, let alone played in a Christian setting. Granted some of the lyrics are so ungodly that you can become completely disgusted. But the fact of the matter is, this is the music that the vast majority of our youth are listening to. If we are going to reach them with the gospel, we have to enter into their world. We must be willing to listen to their music, discuss it with them, expose its empty values, and discover its "hidden message." Beneath the lurid lyrics is a "hidden message" that can liberate their minds and prepare their hearts for the gospel of Jesus Christ.

Therefore, I hope that Christians and people of good will keep an open mind as they use these Liberating Lyrics. I have witnessed their effectiveness amongst youth. Young boys who never went to Sunday school began to eagerly attend because of Liberation Lyrics. Kids who never thought about the Bible began to read it. They enjoyed discussing and reflecting on the songs they listened to. They were open to the meditations that were written about their culture and the will of God. As one young man said, "I like it because it's not boring and I Iearned about God."

Parents can use these Liberating Lyrics to teach their boys biblical truth as it relates to youth perspective. Liberating lyrics will create a dynamic discussion between parent and teen. It foster communication between the generations which will be enlightening for everyone. It is another opportunity for parents to connect to their children and youth. We can share our thoughts and beliefs. My son and I learned a lot about each other. I learned what his favorite rap songs were and why. He learned about my "old school" songs and why I enjoyed them. We did not agree on the meaning of every song but we did agree that it was important to try to understand them.

LIBERATING LYRICS

OPENING PRAYER

SONG: "ALL OF ME"

ARTIST: Drake, 2 Chainz, Big Sean

MEDITATION:

"All me" is a rap song about being honest with yourself and with others. One of the things that every young man should have is integrity. Integrity means being true to yourself and others. It means being honest with your thoughts, feelings and beliefs. "All me" means not being two-faced or a hypocrite. You should not pretend to be something you are not. You should "stay true" to who you are. Often times, people lie to one another. They are not honest. They play games and manipulate one another.

But a real man has integrity and can speak his truth to anyone, anytime and anyplace. A real man can say, "Came up, that's all me. All me for real. Stay true, that's' all me." There is one who had integrity and was honest with himself and others. He lived and spoke the truth. His name is Jesus Christ. Jesus once said, "You will know the truth and the truth will set you free." The truth is that we all have lied or lived a lie and sinned against God. The truth is Jesus Christ died for our sins and was resurrected. If you want to live a life of integrity and have eternal life, Jesus is telling you must accept, "All me".

REFLECTIVE QUESTIONS:

1. Do you like the song? Why or why not?
2. What does the song mean to you and how does it relate to your life?
3. Are you honest with yourself?
4. Are you honest to others? Do you share your true feelings, thoughts and beliefs? Why or why not?
5. Do you share the truth to your family? Why or why not?

6. Do you share the truth to your friends and peers? Why or why not?

7. If you knew someone who committed a crime, would you share the truth to police? Why or why not?

8. Why aren't people honest with each other?

9. Are you willing to accept the truth that Jesus Christ died for your sins and was resurrected? Are you willing to repent of your sins and accept Him as your Lord and Savior?

10. Read the following scriptures on truthfulness and apply them to your life : Proverbs 12:19 , Proverbs 14:25, Zechariah 8:16 , Romans 15:8, John 15:26 , John 14:6 , Psalm 15:1,2 , Hebrews 13:18 , Isaiah 33:15-16

CLOSING PRAYER

LIBERATING LYRICS

OPENING PRAYER

SONG: TEN 2 TEN

ARTIST: Big Shawn

MEDITATION

One of the messages derived from this song is the promotion of the work-ethic. If a person works from 10:00am to 10:00pm then they are working 12 hour days. It takes a lot of commitment, perseverance, and passion to work 12 hour days and 70 hour week. But there is no getting around the fact that the only way you can be a success is hard work. 10 to 10 means you must be willing to roll up your sleeves, burn the midnight hour, and get busy. If you want to do well in school you have to be willing to work hard. If you want to be a successful in life than you must be industrious. If you want to please God you must have faith that works.

REFLECTIVE QUESTION:

1. Do you like this song? Why or why not?
2. What does this song mean to you?
3. How does it apply to your life?
4. Are you willing to work hard to do well in school?
5. Are you willing to work hard to be a success in life? Why or why not?
6. What happens to people who are lazy? Give an example
7. Read the following scriptures and discuss them. Genesis 33:11 ; Psalm 127:1 ; Deut. 8:8-3

CLOSING PRAYER

LIBERATING LYRICS

SONG: FIRST QUARTER

ARTIST: BIG SHAWN

MEDITATION:

The first quarter means that you are just getting started in the game of life. It means that you are just beginning life's journey. There is still a lot for you to do and accomplish. There are battles that need to be fought, mountains that need to be climbed, race that needs to be finished, a game that needs to be won and dreams that need to be fulfilled. You can win life's battles, finish the race and realize your dreams if you,"got a grip, never slip, never panic…not listen and still be on campus." In other words, you must keep your focus and not get side- tracked. You cannot afford to listen to the bad advice of others who would discourage you from pursuing your dreams. You can't listen to those who do not have your best interest in mind. They will hold you back. There are a lot of player haters who don't want you to go forward. They want you to stay "on campus" or remain in the past.

Paul the Apostle was a great missionary who helped build the early Christian church. Moreover he is responsible for writing three-fourths of the New Testament. He preached, taught and faithfully served God. Yet there were those Christians who did not trust him because early in his life he persecuted Christians. Consequently many Christians tried to hold him back and keep him "on the campus". But Paul kept his focus "got a grip, never slipped, never panicked" and continued to do Gods' will. Critics tried to hold him back but Paul stated, "Forgetting those things that are behind, reaching forth I press toward the mark of the high calling in Christ Jesus." Only those who are focused on Gods' will win the ultimate prize of eternal life. You cannot afford to let yourself be sidetracked by player haters, non-believers, negative thinkers and critics. You must keep your grip on the gospel and never slip from doing His will.

REFLECTIVE QUESTIONS:

1. Do you like the song? Why or why not?
2. What does the song mean to you?
3. What are the goals or dreams that you are trying to accomplish?
4. What are some things or people that distract you?
5. What can you do to keep your focus on your goals?
6. What are some temptations that can distract you from your relationship with God?
7. What does it mean to be determined and how can you have it?
8. Read the following scriptures and discuss them: Matthew 4:1-11 , Matthew 16:24-26 , Titus 2:11-12 , James 1:12-14

CLOSING PRAYER

LIBERATING LYRICS

OPENING PRAYER

SONG: BEWARE

ARTIST: Big Shawn

MEDITATION

This song warns us about the dangers of falling in love with the wrong woman. The wrong woman could have a broken heart from a previous relationship and she takes it out on you. The wrong woman may be unfaithful and have multiple lovers. A woman with a broken heart may constantly break your heart. Many men have fallen into a pit of despair because of a broken hearted woman. Many have lost their careers, heart, mind and soul because of a broken hearted woman. There are young men in jail, living in a bottle, addicted to drugs, homeless and hopeless because of a woman. Big Shawn is right," beware of a woman with a broken heart."

REFLECTIVE QUESTIONS:

1. Do you like the song? Why or why not?
2. What does the song mean to you?
3. Can you identify a broken hearted woman?
4. How do you know if a girl is right for you?
5. What kind of personality do you like in a girl?
6. How do you know if a girl is playing games with you?
7. What is the difference between lust and love?
8. How do you know if a girl really loves you?
9. Read the following scriptures I. Thessalonians 4:3,7 , I. Corinthians 7:7,8,25,29,32

CLOSING PRAYER

LIBERATING LYRICS

SONG: Head Lights

ARTIST: M&M

MEDITATION

M&M discloses his dysfunctional relationship with his mother. He shares his broken heart and bitter disappointment in his absent father. M&M shares his hurt and anger. The relationship between a child and their parents should be a sacred, special bond. The healthier the relationship, the healthier and adjusted the child will be. But if the parental bond is ruined it can have a detrimental effect on the child. There are many children who grew up in dysfunctional, abusive families and ended up on drugs, engaged in prostitution, participating in criminal activity and in jail cells. But there are those exceptional persons like M&M who were able to transcend their dysfunctional families past and have a successful future. Your past does not have to determine your destiny. It doesn't matter what kind of family you were raised in, you still can succeed. You mother maybe neglectful and your father maybe abusive or absent but you can still experience love. You may have been raised in a poor neighborhood, attended substandard schools and had no support at home. God can still make you a great success. God can still do miracles through you and with you.

REFLECTIVE QUESTIONS:

1. Do you like the song? Why or why not?
2. What do you think the song means?
3. How do you feel about your mother?
4. How do you feel about your father?
5. How do you feel about your siblings?
6. Have you ever been physically abused? When, why and who did it?
7. Have you ever been verbally abused? When, why and who did it?
8. Have you forgiven your mother, father, and sibling?

9. Can you let go of your past hurts and be thankful for your present blessings?
10. Read the following scriptures Mark 11:25, Matthew 6:14, Matthew 5:44, 45, Luke 6:35-38 and share your thoughts.

CLOSING PRAYER

LIBERATING LYRICS

SONG: How to Love

ARTIST: Lil Wayne

MEDITATION:

One of the most difficult experiences in life is being in a loving relationship. Love can lift you to mountain tops of joy or bring you down to valleys of sadness. Sometimes love hurts. You can be in love and still be rejected, neglected, exploited and alienated. There is only one person who will never break your heart and he is Jesus Christ. He is the lover of your soul and he will never leave you or forsake you. Jesus loves you so much that he was willing to suffer, bleed and die on the cross for your redemption. The bible says, "God so loved the world that he gave his only begotten son, so that whoever believes in him will not perish, but have everlasting life."(John 3:16) The only one who really knows how to love is Jesus Christ. If you want to know what it feels like to be loved, talk to Jesus.

REFLECTIVE QUESTIONS:

1. How do you define love?
2. Have you ever been in love? What happened?
3. Have you ever prayed to God about your broken heart?
4. Have you ever experienced Gods love?
5. Have you repented of your sins and accepted Jesus Christ as Lord and Savior?
6. Read the following scriptures and share how they apply to your life. John13:34-35 , Jeremiah 31:3 , Ephesians 2:4-7 , I. John 4:10,16 , Deut. 11:13-15

CLOSING PRAYER

LIBERATING LYRICS

SONG: Believe me

ARTIST: Lil Wayne, Drake

MEDITATION:

Lil Wayne believes in himself. He believes in his musical ability, talent, skills and charisma to be one of the great rappers of our time. He believes in his ability to entertain millions of listeners. Self-confidence is indispensable to survival and success in any endeavor. You have to learn to believe in yourself, even when others do not. You not only need to believe in yourself, you have to believe in God. You must believe in the God inside of you. God will give you the faith to do the impossible. Like Paul the Apostle you can say, "I can do all things through Christ who strengthens me."(Philippians 4:13)

REFLECTIVE QUESTIONS:

1. Do you like the song? Why or why not?
2. What do you think the meaning of the song is?
3. Do you believe in yourself?
4. What do you have doubts about and why?
5. How does faith in God help you to believe in yourself?
6. Read the following scriptures and apply them to your life. Hebrews 11:1-40

CLOSING PRAYER

LIBERATING LYRICS

OPENING PRAYER

SONG: We made it

ARTIST: Drake

MEDITATION:

According to Drake, he is a great success. His song "We made it" boast his prosperity, property and privileged status. His song brags about his mansion, private jet, and beautiful women. Drake has all the symbols of worldly success. He thinks he "made it" because he is rich.

But the bible teaches us the complete opposite. The bible says, "The love of money is the root of all evil." Furthermore the bible warns us, "Those who want to be rich will fall into many lustful cravings." The bible teaches, "It is more blessed to give than receive." Finally Jesus asks the question, "What does it profit a man that he should gain the whole world and lose his own soul." You may have "made it" according to the worlds standards but not Gods standard. To make it in the eyes of God you must "love him with all your heart, mind, soul and strength and your neighbor as yourself." You can say you made it when you, "confess with your mouth the Lord Jesus and believe in your heart that God raised him from the dead, you will be saved." The only people who can say they truly made it are the ones who have a relationship with Jesus Christ. One day when we are all in heaven we can shout and say, "We made it!"

REFLECTIVE QUESTIONS:

1. Do you like the song? Why or why not?
2. What does the song mean to you?
3. How will you know you are a success?
4. What is the difference between worldly success and spiritual success?

5. Do you give more than you receive? Why or why not?
6. Have you repented of your sins and accepted Christ as your Lord and Savior?

CLOSING PRAYER

LIBERATING LYRICS

SONG: My "n" word

ARTIST: Sha Stimuli aka Yogotty

MEDITATION:

This song talks about the "n" word in African American culture. Far too many African Americans use the "n" word affectionately. They use it the same way as someone would say brother. They don't mean it as an insult but as a term of endearment. Unfortunately, they have forgotten the historical roots to this racial derogatory word. The "n" word was used to oppress, exploit, dehumanize, discriminate and denigrate African Americans. The "n" word was used to tar, feather, emasculate and hang Black men. It was used by slave masters as they whipped their male slaves and rapped their women. The "n" word was used by the rabid segregationists, domestic terrorist, and Klan's men, as they enforced Jim Crow laws with police dogs, water hoses, stoning's, burning crosses, bombing churches, assassination of leaders and mob violence. The "n" word is an evil, ungodly, wicked, sinful word that should never be used by anyone, let alone African Americans.

REFLECTIVE QUESTIONS:

1. Do you like the song? Why or why not?
2. What do you think the song means to you?
3. Do you use the "n" word? Why or why not?
4. How does it make you feel when someone calls you the "n" word?
5. How do you feel when you use the "n" word?
6. Would Jesus use the "n" word? Why or why not?
7. Would you make a commitment not to use the "n" word?
8. Read the following scriptures and discuss how they apply to you. Leviticus 19:16 , Proverbs 18:8 , Psalm 34:13 ,

CLOSING PRAYER

LIBERATING LYRICS

OPENING PRAYER

SONG: LEVELS

ARTIST: Meek Mill

MEDITATION:

One of the issues that Meek addresses in this rap is jealousy. He points out the social stratification that is based on income, power, privilege and property. Not everyone is on the same socio-economic level. Consequently people tend to criticize and be jealous of one another. Jealousy means envying someone else. It means coveting what someone else possess. Jealousy is a sin against Almighty God. There are many people who are jealous of one another. We call them player haters. They are jealous of cars, clothes, jewelry, popularity, women, homes, appearances, status, income and other things. Those who are jealous can become irrational, angry, frustrated, bitter, sad, hateful and spiteful. Jealousy can transform two best friends into two mortal enemies. Jealousy can make people hostile to one another. A jealous person may ignore you, criticize you, put you down and hold you back. Remember the first murder recorded in the Bible, was by jealous Cain who killed his brother Able. Cain murdered Able because he was jealous of his "level". We need not be jealous of each other because God made us all on the same level. We are all equal in the eyes of God. God loves all of His children the same. We maybe have different blessings, but we are all loved the same. Therefore we should not be envious but thankful. We should thank and praise God for whoever we are and whatever we have.

REFLECTIVE QUESTIONS:

1. Do you like the song? Why or why not?
2. What do you think the meaning of the song is?
3. Are you jealous of someone? Why?
4. Is someone jealous of you?

5. Why is jealousy a bad feeling?
6. Do you think that you are better than someone else? Why or why not?
7. Do you think that someone is better than you? Why or why not?
8. Why is bragging and boasting about yourself wrong?
9. What are you thankful to God about?
10. Read the following scriptures and share how they apply to your life. Proverbs 6:34, Genesis 37:1-36 ,

CLOSING PRAYER

LIBERATING LYRICS

OPENING PRAYER

SONG: "I know"

ARTIST: Lil Wayne

MEDITATION:

All throughout the song Lil Wayne shares his street knowledge. He is aware of women who try to use him. He knows about rappers who are jealous of him. He knows all the dangers, toils and snares that await him. Like Lil Wayne we should be able to say,"I know". We should always be aware of our social environment, so-called friends, and temptations. Ignorance is not bliss. You make yourself vulnerable when you ignore the evils of the world. We need to arm ourselves with as much knowledge and wisdom as we can. Learn about what is going on and prepare yourself. The bible reminds us to, "watch as well as pray." We need to watch everything and everybody. We need to know what is going on in life and pray about it. Moreover, we need to know the Lord. The most important person you should know is Jesus Christ. Before you die make sure you can say, "I know, I know, I know the Lord."

REFLECTIVE QUESTIONS

1. Are you aware of the drug activity in your neighborhood or at school? Explain
2. Are you aware of all the dangers of using drugs or alcohol? What are they?
3. Do you know who the drug dealers are and what they are doing?
4. Are you aware of the dangers of being a part of a gang? What are they?
5. Do you know that if you drop out of school you may end doing crime and in jail?

6. Do you know that one-out of four young African American males end up in the criminal justice system? Will you be the one to get arrested? How do you know?

7. Can you tell the difference between your friends and your enemies? Explain

8. Do you know that if you do well in school, go to trade school or college you have a greater chance to succeed in life? What do you want to do?

9. Did you know that if you do poorly in school , don't do homework, get bad grades there is a good chance you will either be poor or in jail? Is this what you want out of life? What will you do about it?

10. Are you aware of your strengths and weaknesses?

11. Did you know that if you engage in premarital sex there is a chance of you getting a s.t.d or getting someone pregnant? Did you know that wearing a condom is not a 100% insurance against unwanted pregnancy or s.t.d?

12. Did you know that Jesus Christ was crucified, dead, buried and was resurrected? Do you know that, "If you confess with your mouth the Lord Jesus and believe in your heart that God raised Him from the dead you will be saved"? Do you know the Lord?

CLOSING PRAYER

LIBERATING LYRICS

OPENING PRAYER

SONG: "Living for the City"

ARTIST: Stevie Wonder

MEDITATION:

Stevie Wonder shares some of the struggles of living in the city. He paints a picture of poverty, injustice, crime and despair. Unfortunately there are far too many of us who are living just enough for the city. There are too many of us barely making the ends meet. We struggle just to eke out an existence. Our children and youth are tempted to do drugs and engage in criminal activity. It's not safe for them to play outside or walk to school. Our seniors are prisoners in their own homes, afraid of the violence that awaits them outside. Our ghetto is filled with abandoned, dilapidated housing. Our streets are filled with garbage, rats, stray dogs and cats. There is prostitution, homelessness and drug dealing on every corner. No matter where you look there is hopelessness and despair.

The good news is that our God has not abandoned or forsaken the city. God sent His son Jesus Christ to live in a poor ghetto called Nazareth. Jesus was raised, lived, preached, taught, healed the sick, fed the hungry and did ministry in the city. Jesus lived in the ghetto but the ghetto was not in him. He never lost his sense of divinity and dignity. He did not let the evils of the city change his holy character. He transcended temptation and did the will of God. Jesus had so much compassion for urban dwellers that he "wept over the city." God has always been committed to those who live just enough for the city. He is there weeping over our cities. He is there watching over you, strengthening you, and providing for you. We may be living for the city, but God is living for us.

REFLECTIVE QUESTIONS:

1. Did you like the song? Why or why not?

2. What do you think the song means?
3. What do you find difficult about living for the city?
4. Where do you see God in the city?
5. What can you do to survive in the city?
6. You can live in the ghetto but not have the ghetto in you. What does that mean?
7. Read the following scriptures and share how they apply to you. Matthew 25:31-46, II. Peter 2:9, I. Corinthians 10:12-13 , I.Peter 5:8,9, James 2:5

CLOSING PRAYER

LIBERATING LYRICS

OPENING PRAYER

SONG: Trouble man

ARTIST: Marvin Gaye

MEDITATION:

Marvin Gaye shares, "I come up hard." In other words nothing came easy for him. Life was one big long struggle. He had to deal with one hardship after another. No one helped him and no one seemed to care. Nor was he able to count on anyone or anything. He was a troubled man. What about you? Are you troubled about something? Are you troubled about money, family, school, friends, girls, parents, drugs, gangs, or police? Are you worried or anxious? Are you angry or frustrated? We all have troubles. The question is how do you handle them?

Our Lord and Savior Jesus Christ says to the troubled, "Come to me all who labor and are heavy burden. And I will give you rest. Take my yoke upon you and learn of me. For my yoke is easy and my burden is light." Jesus offers to take your troubles and burdens. If you pray and talk to Him, He will give you peace of mind. Jesus will give you the grace to handle all your pressures and problems. He will enable you to deal with your troubles. Whatever your troubles, you can take them to the Lord. Job testifies to us, "He shall deliver you in six troubles, yes, in seven no evil shall touch you." (Job 5:19)

REFLECTIVE QUESTIONS:

1. Do you like this song? Why or why not?
2. What does this song mean to you?
3. What are some of the troubles, pressures or burdens that you have?
4. How do you cope with them?
5. Some people cope with their troubles by using drugs or alcohol. Why is this bad for you?

6. Read the following scriptures and share how they apply to your life? Psalm 46:1 ,I Corinthians 12:9 ; Philippians 4:6-7 ; John 14:27 ; Isaiah 26:3

CLOSING PRAYER

Dr. Samuel White, III

LIBERATING LYRICS

OPENING PRAYER

SONG: Get up, Stand up

ARTIST: Bob Marley

MEDITATIONS:

Bob Marley points out the hypocrisy of the church that focuses on Heavenly reward and ignores earthly injustices. He pleads to the masses to stand up for their rights. It is the will of God for oppressed people to pray, preach, protest, and non-violently fight for their social, economic, and political rights. The bible commands us to, "Do justice, love mercy and walk humbly with our God." We need to stand up for our rights like Moses did before Pharoah and say, "Let my people Go." Stand up for your rights like the Old Testament prophets, "who let justice roll down like waters and righteousness like a mighty flowing stream." Stand up for their rights like our Lord who said,"The Spirit of the Lord is upon me to preach the gospel to the poor and set at liberty them that are bruised." Every child of God has a moral responsibility to "Get up, Stand up for your rights."

REFLECTIVE QUESTIONS:

1. Do you like this song? Why or why not?
2. What does this song mean to you?
3. Are you willing to stand up for your rights? Share a time when you stood up for your rights.
4. Have you ever stood up for the rights of someone else? Give an example.
5. What or who are you willing to fight for?
6. Why don't people stand up for themselves?
7. Can you fight for yourself without being violent?

8. What are the ways you can fight without using knives, guns, fists etc.?

9. Read the following scriptures and share how they apply to your life. Psalm 72:1-4 ; Isaiah 1:17 ; Isaiah 58:1-9 ; Luke 4:18,19

CLOSING PRAYER

LIBERATING LYRICS

OPENING PRAYER

SONG: One Love

ARTIST: Bob Marley

MEDITATION:

Bob Marley sings about the need to have more unity and amity among all people. He shares that there needs to be one love, one heart. He emphasizes that it is Gods' will that sinner and saint must come together before the judgment of God. We need to love and respect one another. We should not let our differences keep us from worshipping All Mighty God who can unify us as one family. We should not let our race, class, gender, political perspectives, worship style, ethnic background or personal issues separate us from each other. The tie that binds us is our relationship with God through His son Jesus Christ. It is through Christ that we are brothers and sisters. It is in Him that we are family.

REFLECTIVE QUESTIONS:

1. Do you like the song? Why or why not?
2. What does this song mean to you?
3. What are some of the reasons people are not unified? Or why are we divided?
4. How can you show unity to someone you do not like?
5. Are there certain kind of people you do not like?
6. How do you feel when people disrespect you or discriminate against you?
7. What do you think that God thinks of bigotry, prejudice and discrimination?
8. How can you bring more unity to your home?
9. How can you bring more unity to your school?

10. How can you bring more unity to your neighborhood?
11. Read the following scriptures and discuss them : John 13:34-35 ; Romans 12:9-10 ; I. John 4:7-8 ; Colossians 3:12-13

CLOSING PRAYER

LIBERATING LYRICS

OPENING PRAYER

SONG: Shining Star

ARTIST: Earth, Wind and Fire

MEDITATION:

Earth, Wind and Fire sing about the infinite potential and possibilities that are within every human being. Each of us is a shining star because our God has created us. We are all made in the" image of God" and it is that divine spark in us that can lift us to great heights. It's the shining star within us that gives us the faith in ourselves to do the impossible. Paul the Apostle, acknowledged the shining star and was able to say," I can do all things through Christ who strengthens me." You are a shining star and with God there is nothing you can't do.

REFLECTIVE QUESTIONS:

1. Do you like the song? Why or why not?
2. What do you think the song means?
3. Do you feel like a shining star? Why or why not?
4. What makes you so special?
5. What are your gifts and talents?
6. What are your dreams and goals in life?
7. What do you want to be when you grow up?
8. What is your vision of the future?
9. What do you have to do to make your dreams come true?
10. Read the following scriptures and discuss them: I. John 5:4; Isaiah 62:2-3; Isaiah 41:10; Philippians 1:6; II. Corinthians 4:8,9

CLOSING PRAYER

LIBERATING LYRICS

OPENING PRAYER

SONG: Everyday

ARTIST: Chief Keef,

MEDITATION

Every day for Sosa is a party. Every day is an opportunity for him to get high and have premarital sex. Sosa thinks that it's all about having a good time. He is a true hedonist. A hedonist is a pleasure seeker who fulfills the lust and caprices of the flesh. Every day they seek ways to enjoy life and avoid pain. There are a lot of people like Sosa. They measure every day, everything and everybody by whether it will bring them pain or pleasure. But there was one who lived sacrificially in service to others. Jesus cared more about the needs of the destitute, downtrodden and discriminated than his own. He do not live for himself, he lived for others. Jesus loved you and I so much that he was willing to suffer pain and agony on the cross for our redemption. Every day that you live is because of the grace and mercy of God. Jesus told us how to live every day. He said, "Deny yourself, take up the cross daily and follow me." According to Jesus, every day we should deny ourselves of worldly pleasures and treasures. Every day we should take up our cross or ignore our pain and needs. Every day is an opportunity to follow Jesus Christ and serve others. To follow Christ is the greatest pleasure of them all. He gives us joy that the world can't give or receive.

REFLECTIVE QUESTIONS:

1. Do you like the song? Why or why not?
2. What do you think the song means?
3. What do you think about getting high or drunk?
4. What do you think about denying yourself and serving others?
5. Are you willing to put the needs of others before you? Why or why not?

6. What do you think about the fact that Jesus suffered, bled and died for you?
7. Read the following scriptures and share what how it applies to your life: Mark 12:30-31; I.Peter 3:8, 9

CLOSING PRAYER

LIBERATING LYRICS

OPENING PRAYER

SONG: 3 Hunna

ARTIST: Chief Keef

MEDITATION:

This rap song is about gang violence which is an epidemic in the Black community. There are too many guns available in the city. There are too many young people participating in gangs and use violence to settle their differences. Every day someone is being maimed or killed. Every day some innocent little child is being killed by random gun violence. These gangs are domestic terrorist that have made our city streets a war zone. It's not safe to walk the street. It's not even safe for kids to play outside of their home. We need to heed the words of the Prince of Peace who said, "He that lives by the sword, shall perish by the sword." It is time for us to get stronger gun laws and remove these guns. It's time for us to talk to gang leaders about ending the violence. It's time that we provide employment opportunities and recreational activities for our young people. Our churches, temples and public schools need to teach them anger management and conflict resolution skills. If we are serious about ending gang violence we must make changes individually and institutionally.

REFLECTIVE QUESTIONS:

1. Do you like the song? Why or why not?
2. What do you think the song means?
3. What do you think about gangs?
4. What do you think about guns?
5. What do you think about the gun violence in the community?
6. What can be done about the gun violence?

7. What do you think of the statement, "He that lives by the sword will die by the sword."

8. Read the following scriptures: John14:27; Romans 14:17-19; Romans 12:19-21;Ephesians 3:31-32

CLOSING PRAYER

LIBERATING LYRICS

OPENING PRAYER:

SONG: Diamonds

ARTIST: Chief Keef

MEDITATION:

Chief Keef brags about his diamonds , expensive cars , popularity and prosperity. He believes that his prosperity and privileges make women love him and men hate him. He doesn't realize that his diamonds cannot buy love. Diamonds may make people admire him, follow him, and almost worship him. But they can't make people love him. Only God loves us unconditionally. God loves us with diamonds or without them. He loves rich, poor, saint and sinner. The bible says, "God so loved the world that He gave His only begotten son so that whoever believes in him, would not perish but have everlasting life." (John 3:16) God sees you and I as His "diamond in the rough." Each of us is a precious treasure in the eyes of God. Therefore there is nothing He will not do for us.

REFLECTIVE QUESTIONS:

1. Do you like the song? Why or why not?
2. What do you think the song means?
3. What do you think about people who have a lot of money?
4. What do you think about people who are really poor?
5. Do you admire people who have a lot of things? Why or why not?
6. Do you think God judges us on how much we have or give? Explain
7. What do you think about God loving you unconditionally?
8. Read the following scriptures and discuss them: Psalm 72:12-13 ; Psalm 113:7 ; James 2:1-17

CLOSING PRAYER

Dr. Samuel White, III

LIBERATING LYRICS

OPENING PRAYER

SONG: Hate Bein Sober

ARTIST: Chief Keef

MEDITATION :

Chief Keef says he hates being sober. He would rather be high or drunk than face life's harsh realities. For Chief Keef and many others getting high is a way of life. It enables them to deal with life's challenges. They hate being sober. They dislike confronting the problems and pressures of life. Getting high or drunk is an escape from reality. Unfortunately there is no escaping reality. The bottle or a joint may bring temporary relief but you still have to deal with your issues. The bible teaches us that we can get high in the spirit and face our problems. Getting high in the Holy Ghost means to surrender yourself to the presence of God. It means to "be filled in the Spirit." (Ephesians 5:18-20) If you really want to get high, begin to pray, sing, praise and worship Him. If you worship Him in Spirit and truth you'll be drunk in the spirit. You will be able to face reality with joy in your heart and peace of mind. You can be high in the spirit and still face reality.

REFLECTIVE QUESTIONS:

1. Do you like the song? Why or why not?
2. What do you think the song means?
3. Have you ever gotten high? Why or why not?
4. Have you ever gotten drunk? Why or why not?
5. What do you do to escape your problems?
6. Have you ever talked to God about your pressures or problems?
7. Have you ever been"drunk in the spirit"?
8. Read the following scriptures and discuss them: Acts 2: 12-21 ; Ephesians 5:18-20

CLOSING PRAYER

LIBERATING LYRICS

OPENING PRAYER

SONG: Love Sosa

ARTIST: Chief Keef

MEDITATION:

This song is about gang violence. There are some young men who participate in gangs that sell drugs, engage in criminal activity and kill people. Some boys do evil without any conscience. They sell drugs and do not care what happens to the drug addict. They murder other boys and don't care about the victim's family. They rob and steal from hard working people. They shoot their guns and don't care who gets hit by the bullets. Innocent children are dying and mothers are crying. This is not the way God wants us to live. He did not create us to kill one another. Some say gangs provide a sense of security and family. But the truth is gang members are vulnerable to rival gangs and police. They are not safe, secure havens. Any song that glorifies gang violence like Love Sosa is misleading and evil. We should oppose any song, video, and way of life, behavior or act of violence that perpetuates or promulgates gang culture. Gangs are destroying lives, fragmenting families, terrorizing our neighborhoods and enslaving our boys. We should do everything in our power to end the gangs in our neighborhood.

REFLECTIVE QUESTIONS:

1. Do you like the song? Why or why not?
2. What do you think the song means?
3. What do you think of gangs?
4. Are you in a gang or have you ever been in a gang?
5. What do you like about being in a gang?
6. What do you don't' like about it?
7. What could the church do to end gangs?

8. What could you do to end gangs?
9. Read the following scriptures and discuss them: Romans 8:37-39 ; Isaiah 43:2 ; John14:27

CLOSING PRAYER

LIBERATING LYRICS

OPENING PRAYER:

SONG: Trophies

ARTIST: Drake

MEDITATION:

There are some people who do humanitarian and philanthropic work to be rewarded, recognized, and praised by others. In fact some people will not do a good deed, unless they can be recognized in some way. Some people will even get angry and upset when they are not appreciated and acknowledged. But Drake makes an excellent point. He doesn't look for any "trophies" or rewards for taking care of his people. He is not seeking "award" for doing what he is supposed to do. Our world would change overnight if people began to help others without reward. They only "trophy" we should seek is the inner satisfaction that we have given our best. The only "reward" that we should be concerned about is the one we will get in heaven.

REFLECTIVE QUESTIONS:

1. Do you like the song? Why or why not?
2. What do you think the song means?
3. Why do you do good deeds?
4. How do you feel when people do not say "thank you?"
5. How do you feel when people do not recognize or reward you?
6. What are some good things you can do for your family?
7. What are some good things you could do for your friends?
8. What are some good things you could do for poor and needy people?
9. Read the following scriptures and discuss them: Psalm 41:1-2 ; Proverbs 19:17 ; Luke 14:13,14 ; Luke 12:33 ; Proverbs 14:21

CLOSING PRAYER

LIBERATING LYRICS

OPENING PRAYER

SONG: Wit me

ARTIST: T.I

MEDITATION :

T.I. sings about having friends, family, streets, drugs, alcohol with him. These things give him a sense of security. He feels strong because his love ones are with him. They have his back. He feels secure because he has all of his creature comforts with him. The rocks, alcohol make him feel good and comfortable. But what T.I does not realize is that everlasting security can only come with your relationship with God. When you realize that God is with you and will never abandon you, you really have a sense of security. Family and friends can be fickle. The streets can be threatening and dangerous. Drugs and alcohol can make you vulnerable. The only one you can count on in this life and beyond is God. He is with me and with you. You are never alone as long as you are with God.

REFLECTIVE QUESTIONS:

1. Do you like the song? Why or why not?
2. What do you think the song means?
3. What or who do you need to feel secure?
4. Do you have a relationship with God? Why or why not?
5. What can you do to enhance your relationship with God ?
6. Read the following scriptures and discuss them: John 17:21-23 ; Eccles.4:9-10 ; John 14:18 ; II.Corinthians 6:18 ; Genesis 28:15

CLOSING PRAYER

LIBERATING LYRICS

OPENING PRAYER

SONG: Ball

ARTIST: T.I.

MEDITATION:

T.I. sings about the Ball, the party life, the good times. All throughout the song he talks about getting drunk, high and being with a lot of women. He enjoys going out to the club and partying. T.I is not the only one. There are a lot of people who live to go to the club and Ball. All they think about is going to the club. They work, get paid, buy nice clothes, and get their hair done to go to the club. They go to the club to feel good and get high. They go to the club to meet someone and possibly fall in love. They go to the club to spend their money. They go to club to get away from all the pressures and problems of the world. But what they do not realize is going to the club does not compare to going to the church. The church may not be packed with people but it is full of the Holy Ghost. It is the Holy Ghost that gets the people of God high in the Spirit. In the church we dance, we sing, we praise God about His goodness and mercy. We don't need alcohol, molly, blunts or models to feel good. All we need is the Lord. He is our Holy Ghost party. He is our joy. He is our praise and glory. Some would go to the club. But the people of God can say like the psalmist, "I was glad when they said unto me let us go into the House of the Lord."

REFLECTIVE QUESTIONS:

1. Do you like this song? Why or why not?
2. What do you think this song means?
3. What do you think going to the club is like?
4. What do you think going to the church is like?
5. How do the two compare?
6. What does it mean to be high in the spirit?

7. What are the dangers to getting drunk or high?
8. Read the following scriptures and discuss them: Psalm118:15 ; Psalm97:11-12 ; Psalm 16:11 John 16:20 ; Psalm 68:3

CLOSING PRAYER

LIBERATING LYRICS

OPENING PRAYER

SONG: Made man

ARTIST: Rick Ross

MEDITATION:

Dollar bills, money, cash, Benjamin's, moula, payola, has many names. It really does not matter what we call it, we all want it. We all want a lot of dollar bills. Some of us work hard for them. Some people will lie, cheat, rob and even kill for them. A women will sell her precious body for dollar bills. Boys will sell drugs to one another and rob their own mothers for dollar bills. Everybody wants dollar bills. The problem is "the love of money is the root of all evil." It's the love of dollar bills that makes people do evil and condemn their souls. There is nothing wrong with wanting dollar bills to care for yourself, family and those in need. But if we love money and material things more than we love God and others then we jeopardize our souls.

REFLECTIVE QUESTIONS:

1. Do you like the song? Why or why not?
2. What does the song mean to you?
3. What do you think of money?
4. Do you want to have a lot of money and be rich?
5. If you had a million tax free dollars what would you do?
6. Would you commit a crime to get things that you want? Why or why not?
7. Read the following scriptures and discuss them: Psalm 113:7 ; Psalm 68:10 ; Luke 22:1-6 ; II.Peter 2:3 ; Eccles. 1:8 ; Eccles. 5:10 ; Luke 16:19-31

CLOSING PRAYER

Chapter Eight

Liberating Parents

"Fathers do not anger your children, or they will become discouraged." Colossians 3:21

There are a lot of great parents with bad kids. There are parents who are holy and their children still give them a hard time. They prayed for them ,taught them, brought them to Sunday school and worship service and their boys end up high school drop outs, gangsters and drug addicts. A parent can do all the right things and their children still end up wrong. I can think of many single good Christian women who raised, disciplined and taught their sons in a Christian environment and their boys ended up in jail. What happened? Who is at fault? As I indicated in the earlier chapters the social environment, criminal culture, peer pressure, poor public schools, gangs, drug dealers, corrupt media and co- dependent churches all play a role in the down fall of our youth. But parents must also share some responsibility in the moral failures of their children.

One of the ways that young African American males are liberated is through their parents. If Parents are truly saved and there is a good chance that their children will be saved. Christian Parents can teach their children the plan of salvation in Christ and how to live the Christian life. Christian parenting is an integral part of the liberation process of children and youth. A child learns firsthand what it is to be a Christian and to be free in the spirit. Raising a child in a Christian environment makes a fundamental difference in their moral and spiritual development. A child learns from a biblical perspective what is right and what is wrong. They learn who Jesus Christ is and how He can liberate you from your sins. Christian parents can raise the self-esteem of their children by reminding them of their divine identity. They will learn that they are children of God and "can do all things through Christ who strengthens [them]." Philippians 4:13

If parents do not believe in Jesus Christ as Lord and Savior or don't live out the gospel, they put their childrens' soul in jeopardy. A non-practicing Christian parent may not realize it but they are part of the problem. A refusal or neglect to teach your child the gospel of Jesus Christ may mean their psychological and spiritual bondage. A child may become enslaved to the wicked ways of the world. If we do not teach our children right from wrong, the streets will teach them. Every child needs to be taught the gospel from their parents. They need to see the manifestation of the gospel in the lifestyle of their parents. Its' not enough to send your children to Sunday school and not study the bible with them. It's not enough for parents to make perfunctory prayers over the dinner table and attend church on Easter, Mother's Day, Christmas and other special days. It's not enough for parents to say they believe in Jesus Christ and the bible. They must practice what they preach. They must have faith and works. It's not just what a parent says that's important, it's what they do. For our children and youth learn more by what we do than what we say.

One of the things that children and youth learn is the lies that we parents tell ourselves. Too many parents are enslaved to parenting lies and half-truths that make them ineffective parents. Consequently, many parents feel frustrated, angry, depressed and hopeless. They need the Lord to liberate them psychologically and spiritually from a symbiotic relationship with their wayward son.

Many parents need to be liberated from their co-dependent behavior. They believed the lie that they can control their troubled teenager. They think that if they yell, scream, and scold their boys they will control them. They mistakenly think that they can change their boy's behavior. But if we are honest with ourselves we will admit that it is impossible to control our teenager. He may act sweet and innocent in the home but be a terror on the streets. He may modify the way he acts around you but not really change the way he thinks and feels. Those of us who think that we can play God with our children, are in for a rude awakening. If our sons are to be liberated we must be liberated. We must be liberated from the notion that we can change our sons. Only God can change our sons' heart, mind and soul. We are co-laborers in their liberation process but it is God who does the work. We must surrender our sons to the Lord. Just as Abraham was willing to sacrifice his son Isaac to the Lord, we must surrender our sons to the Lord.

Some parents need to be liberated spiritually from themselves. Their pride and arrogance makes them think that they do not need the Lord or obey the Word of God for themselves. Many parents think they can raise their children without the guidance of the Lord. They want to be good parents but refuse to read the good book, the bible. The bible is a parents manual on how to raise their children. The Holy Scriptures are full wisdom and can enlighten parents on what to do and what not to do.

Then there are some parents who think they can preach the gospel to their kids and not live the gospel. Their pride makes them think that they don't need to change their ways. They don't realize that if they don't change, it will be hard for their boys to change. Parents can't' liberate their sons, if they aren't liberated. If parents are using profanity, drinking alcohol, getting high, fighting and not living holy lifestyle then they can't expect their sons to change their baneful behavior. If a parent is setting a bad example, how can they expect their teen to do any better? The first person who needs to repent in the parent/child relationship is the parent. The parent must repent of their personal sins and get right with God. They must repent of their parenting dysfunctions and work on a biblically based relationship with their sons.

The key to liberating parents is found in the Holy Scriptures. The bible is replete with examples of good and bad parents that we may learn from. The Old Testament is one saga after another of families struggling to survive and keeping the faith. In many instances, biblical families are a lot like our families. They struggled with broken relationships, adultery, incest, unfaithfulness, drunkenness and ungodliness. The only difference between biblical families and contemporary families is faith. The biblical families were not more holy but they may have had more faith. It was their faith in God that saved them and liberated them.

If todays' family is to be liberated, they must make faith in God their number one priority. The bible says "without faith it's impossible to please God." The bible also says, "Faith cometh by hearing, and hearing by the word of God." Therefore, parents must read and obey the Word of God which will increase their faith. The parents will then have the faith to raise their sons with the right spiritual perspective. Also reading the bible will give a Christian parent the wisdom and insight they need. They will be set free from lies and half-truths that inevitably make them ineffective, dysfunctional parents. There are ten parenting dysfunctions that parents need to be aware of.

TEN PARENTING DYSFUNCTIONS

PARENT DYSFUNCTION # 1 – LACK OF PRAYER

Parents think that they can raise their children without the power of prayer. Far too many parents do not pray daily. Parents need to seek the Lords will for their child through prayer. Begin to pray with your child in the name of Jesus and have faith that God answers prayer. Pray that you can become a better parent. Ask God to give you the wisdom to say and do the right thing. Set aside a special time for the family to pray together. Show your son how to pray for himself and others. Pray even if your teenager refuses to pray with you. He needs to know about the power of prayer. Read Matthew 7:7-8; I. John 5:14-15; Jeremiah 33:3 about the power of prayer.

PARENT DYSFUNCTION #2 – UNGODLY LIFE STYLE

Parents think that their immoral, ungodly lifestyle or behavior does not impact a child's behavior. Our children and youth are impacted more by what we do than what we say. Children and youth are always listening and watching us. They are observing all of our bad habits, vices and weaknesses. Parents must change their ways if they want their boys to change. Parents must set an example for their children. Change begins at the top. Begin to pray to God to help you with your bad habits, vices and weaknesses. Ask God to help you to be a better parent. Read Romans 12:1-2; II. Chronicles 7:14; Luke 3:8; Matthew 5:13-16 on repentance and renewal.

PARENT DYSFUNCTION #3- SPEAKING NEGATIVELY

Parents should not use demeaning names or constantly criticize their children. It is a sin against God and erodes a child's self-esteem. Every time you call your son a negative name or harshly criticizing him you are slowly breaking his spirit. The words that you use have the power to make or break your child. Parents must speak positively to their children. They must refrain from name calling or belittling their children. Begin to watch what you say around your child and speak positively. Compliment your child when they are doing something well. Emphasize the things that they are doing right rather than the things they are doing wrong. Parents must validate the divinity that is in their child which will build their self –esteem. Remind them that God loves them and will never abandon them. Read James 3:1-13 ; Leviticus 19:16 ; Proverbs 18:8 ; Psalm34:13 Psalm 52:2 ; Proverbs 20:19 ; Romans 8:14-18 ; Galatians 3:26 ; I. John 3:1-2 ; Romans 9:26 ; Isaiah 54:13 ; Mark 10:14-16 about the power of words.

PARENT DYSFUNCTION #4-BIBLICAL ILLITERACY

Parents who do not read the bible, refuse to obey it or teach it are really harming themselves and their children. I firmly believe that this is one of the major problems in some of our families. Our lack of spiritual knowledge and neglect in teaching our children has created a moral, social crises. Biblical illiteracy is injurious to the parent because it means a lack of faith. The bible says, "Faith cometh by hearing and hearing by the word of God." If a parent does not read the bible daily they will not have enough faith to raise their child. It takes a lot of faith to raise a good child, let alone a bad one. Parents must make the reading of the bible a priority in their life. They should spend quality time studying the Word of God. (II. Timothy 2:15) As they study their faith and parental wisdom will increase. Moreover every parent is mandated by God to teach His word. The bible emphasizes the responsibility of parents to instruct them in the ways of the Lord. (Deuteronomy 6:4-9) Parent should constantly teach their children about God and how they must be obedient to God. (Deuteronomy 4:9-10) Parents are to be a living witness of what the Lord has done. They need to tell their children how the Lord has blessed them. They need to tell their own story of a good and great God. (Psalm 78:2-8)The failure to teach our children Gods word is partly evident in the godless, self-destructive behavior of our youth. (Jeremiah 9:14) Parents need to take time out of their busy schedules and read the Bible and share it with their children. The Liberation lessons in this book are excellent bible studies for parents to learn and teach their sons. Read II.Timothy 2:15; II.Chronicles 5:7; Hebrews 11 and Deuteronomy 11:19

PARENT DYSFUNCTION #5- GIVING UP HOPE

Parents should never give up or totally reject their troubled teenager because of criminal activity, addictive behavior, or belligerent, antiauthoritarian attitude. The truth is no child is beyond the grace of God to forgive and change. God can change anyone and anytime. We may give up on our children, but God never does. Parents need to place all their faith and hope in God. Never give up. God can still do a miracle in your son. Read the following scriptures: II.Peter 1:9; I. Corinthians 10:13; Psalm27:14; Hebrews 2:18; Hebrews 11:6; Matthew 8:8-10

PARENT DYSFUNCTION #6-OVER CONTROLLING

Parents need to be liberated from being over controlling and believing they can change their child or youth. Only God can change the heart, mind and soul of an individual. The only one a parent can change is themselves. Instead of always focusing on the wrong doings of their child, they need to reexamine their own lives. Parents need to learn how to surrender their sons to the Lord. As Hannah surrendered her son to God, so must every

217

mother surrender their son. Let go and let God correct, consecrate, and change your son. Read the following scriptures: Deuteronomy 30:15-16; Matthew 7:21-25; Philippians 4:9; James 1:25; Psalm106:3

PARENT DYSFUNCTION #7- HAVING FAITH AND NOT WORKS

Parents think that all they need to do is pray for their child and not work with their child. They think that if they have faith, God will do a miracle. But the bible reminds us that "faith without works is dead."(James 2:26) It takes more than prayer to transform a teen. It takes counseling, setting a moral example, diligent study of the Bible, constant mentoring and active participation in a youth ministry to change a young man. Read the following scriptures: Deuteronomy 28:12; II. Chronicles 15:7; I. Corinthians 15:58; I. Thessalonians 4:11-12; Hebrews 6:10-11; Proverbs 14:13

PARENT DYSFUNCTION #8-NOT SEEKING GODS VISION FOR YOUR SON

Parents must liberate themselves from their hopes and dreams for their children. They are not supposed to superimpose their vision on their children. Parents need to assist their sons in helping them discover their God given gifts and their vision for their life. It is the role of the parent to help their young men develop a vision for themselves. The bible says, "… your young men shall see visions…" (Acts 2:17) Notice it does not state, "parents shall see visions for their young men." But it is the young men who have been given a vision. Parents don't give the vision, God gives the vision. They pray for and with their sons to discover their vision. Once a child discovers their purpose in life, the parent helps them to fulfill it. Read the following scriptures: Habakkuk 2:2;

PARENT DYSFUNCTION #9-NOT TAKING FULL RESPONSIBILITY FOR YOUR SON

Parents mistakenly think that the teacher, the preacher, mentor, or youth worker are responsible for their sons intellectual, social and spiritual development. The parent is the primary person who is responsible for their son's growth. They should not be overly dependent on individuals or institutions to raise their sons. The parent must spend quality time talking with their son. It's really up to the parent to be there for their son. They should be the one to teach their sons right from wrong. They should be the ones warning them about the dangers of premarital sex, drugs, and peer pressure and gang violence. It's up to the parent to be their son's primary mentor and telling them how to cope with life's challenges. Parent must not let anything or anyone deter, discourage or deny them of fulfilling their parental responsibilities. Read

PARENT DYSFUNCTION #10-NOT CLOSELY MONITOURING YOUR SON

Parents think that they can let their sons spend hours watching violent video games and listening to lurid lyrics in rap music and not have an effect on them. Scientific studies have revealed that listening to Rap music and watching violent video games will impact how a young man thinks and what he believes. It will desensitize him of violence and possibly corrupt his character. Parents need to closely monitor what their teens are watching and listening to. Sit down with your young man and listen to his music and discuss it. Look at his text messages and see what he is talking about. Read his lap top and discover what his interest are. Get into his life and see what he thinking. Who are the people he is texting and what are they saying to each other? You can not allow your son to live without any direct instruction and influence from you. You must be thoroughly involved in every aspect of his life. You need to know who his friends are, where he goes, what he does, how he is doing in school and what his future plans are. The Liberating Lyrics in this book can be used by parent to open the door toward communication. Discussing the meaning of his favorite rap songs is a great way to develop a meaningful dialogue about what he thinks, feels and copes with.

These ten parenting dysfunction are the issues that parents can acknowledge and ask God to help them with. What is important is that you recognize your faults, repent and do something about it. There is no such thing as a perfect parent. We all have faults. We all have issues that we are struggling with. But if we are honest with ourselves and repent of our dysfunctions, God is able to do a great work in us. God can liberate us that we might be able to liberate our sons.

PROFILES IN PARENTING

Parents in the Bible were neither good nor evil. They were human. Like us they had their strengths and their weaknesses. They were holy men and women of God but they still made a lot of mistakes. We can learn from their mistakes. We can learn what to do and what not to do. The bible provides us profiles of parents that will teach us how to be better parents. Biblical fathers like Adam, Abraham, Jacob, David and Joseph all give us pearls of wisdom. Also ancient mothers like Rebekah, Jochebed, Bathsheba and Mary can inform today's mother. There will be a brief summary of these parents and a lesson that we can learn from them. Moreover we will ask reflective questions that will stimulate deeper thinking and encourage more action.

FATHER ADAM

Adam was the first father that ever lived. Adam was disobedient and sinned against God. Consequently, we all became sinners and have fallen short of the glory of God. His two sons Cain and Able were born in iniquity. Cain was jealous and murdered his brother Able. What is most disturbing is that there is no record of Adams intervention before, during or after the tragic murder of his son. Surely Adam must have seen the growing hostility between his two sons. Why didn't he bring them together? Why didn't he prevent this tragedy from happening? He could have had them discuss their feelings and differences. And where was Adam after his son was killed? Was he grieving the death of Able and the fugitive status of Cain? Did he seek his son Cain? Where was Adam when his family was falling apart? Does he bear some responsibility in raising a son who was a cold bloodied killer?

The overall sin of Adam is that he was an absent father. He was not there when he sons needed him the most. What about you? Are you emotionally, physically absent from your son? Are you physically and emotionally present for your son? Are you there for him to discuss his feelings? Do you allow him to vent his anger and frustration? Do you know how your son is feeling? Is he harboring hostility toward someone? Is there any sibling rivalry in your home? Have you taught your son how to resolve conflict peaceably? Are you raising a peacemaker or a trouble maker? Are you unwittingly raising a killer, a thug in your home?

If you are unable to answer these questions than you maybe an absent Father like Adam. It may be only a matter of time before your son becomes Cain and takes his anger out on others. To ensure that this does not happen, I suggest you do the following:

1. Spend quality time with your son. Schedule the time with him and make sure you keep your appointment with him. Never be too busy to not be with your son.
2. Allow your son the opportunity to share his real feelings. Let him share his anger, frustration, hopes and dreams. Do not cut him off if he says something that you do not want to hear. Let him speak his mind.
3. Teach your son how to deal with conflict peaceably. Show him how to agree to disagree. Tell him the importance of learning how to turn the other cheek or be forgiving.
4. Tell and show your son how much you love him. Look him in the eye and tell him that you love him. He really wants to know and hear how much he is loved. Don't assume he knows how you feel. Tell him how you feel.
5. Teach your son how to manage his anger. Remind him that he does not have to be dictated by his feelings. Let him know he has a choice in how he responds to life.
6. Participate in different activities with your son. Play video games with him, discuss his music, play ball with him, take him out to breakfast, go fishing , read the bible together, take him to the movies, go to church together, watch T.V. with him and always say a prayer with or for him.
7. Assist your son in his educational pursuits. Help him with his homework , get him vocational training, get a tutor , go to his

school , talk to his teachers, take him to the library , help him prepare for his S.A.T and check out colleges.

8. Assist your son in getting a job. Prepare him for a job interview. If it is possible take him to work with you. Show or tell him what it takes to pay the bills.

9. Ask him about his personal life. Read his text messages and emails. Let him know that you are there and you care.

10. Help your son to discover his vision and purpose in life. Encourage him to pursue his dreams.

REFLECTIVE QUESTIONS:

1. WHAT ELSE COULD YOU DO TO GET INTO YOUR SONS LIFE?

2. HOW COULD YOU DEMONSTRATE YOUR LOVE TO YOUR SON?

3. DO YOU KNOW HOW YOUR SON FEELS?

4. WHAT OTHER ACTIVITIES COULD YOU DO WITH YOUR SON?

5. DO YOU KNOW YOUR SONS FAVOURITE SONGS, HAVE YOU LISTENED TO THEM WITH HIM AND HAVE YOU DISCUSSED THE MEANING OF THOSE SONGS? WHY OR WHY NOT?

6. HAVE YOU TAUGHT YOUR SON HOW TO MANAGE HIS ANGER?

7. HAVE YOU TAUGHT YOUR SON HOW TO RESOLVE CONFLICT?

8. HAVE YOU DEALT WITH SIBLING RIVALRY IN THE HOME?

9. HAVE YOU PRAYED TO GOD AND ASKED HIM HOW TO HANDLE THE SITUATION?

FATHER ABRAHAM

Abraham was not only a biological father, he was a spiritual father. God had given him a vision that he would be father of a nation. The problem was he and his wife Sarah were too old to have children. Abraham did not believe the vision and Sarah laughed at it. Consequently, Abraham and Sarah decided to have their servant procreate with Abraham and had a son named Ishmael. Sarah felt threatened by Abraham's mistress and had her and her son thrown out into the wilderness. Abraham did not fight for his son Ishmael and Ishmael almost ended up dying in the wilderness. What do we learn from Father Abraham's relationship with his son Ishmael? There are several points we learn from this experience.

1. Abraham should have never neglected or rejected his son Ishmael. He should have defended his right to receive love and the basic necessities of life. If you have a child out of wedlock or from a previous marriage you are still morally responsible for that child. You cannot let your spouse, girl friend or ex-girlfriend keep you from loving and caring for your child. Every child deserves to know who their father is and be loved by him.
2. There was a blemish on Ishmael's character because he was born out of wed lock. But there are no illegitimate children, only illegitimate parents. No parent should reject their own flesh and blood. Abraham should have demonstrated to Ishmael that he was just as important as his step brother Isaac. Fathers must share their love to all of their children. Treat all of your children the same. They deserve and need to be loved.

Abraham and Sarah eventually did have their own son named Isaac. But God asked Abraham to sacrifice his only begotten Son Isaac. Abraham took his son Isaac up the mountain and was about to sacrifice him. At the last minute, God told Abraham not to sacrifice his son. God provided a ram in the bush for his sacrifice. What do we learn from father Abraham and his relationship with his son Isaac?

1. Abraham had made God first in His life. Every father must learn that his primary relationship is to His God and then his family. We must put Jesus Christ first in our life. Nothing and no one is more important than our relationship with God and doing His will. Read Matthew 6:33 ; Matthew 10:34-39

2. Abraham worshipped God with his son. Every father must worship God with his son. Fathers must take time out of their busy schedules and go to church. It is not enough to send your son to church with his mother. Your son needs to see you in church worshipping our God.

3. Abraham was obedient to the voice of God. God spoke to him before and after the sacrifice. God told Abraham what to do with his son and Abraham was obedient. Fathers must heed the voice of God and be led by His Holy Spirit. God will not lead you wrong. He will tell you what to do with your son. Pray and ask God for guidance. Ask God to help you be a good father. He will answer your prayers.

4. Abraham did not hurt or kill his son. God did not let Abraham sacrifice his son. The lesson learned is Fathers must discipline their son, but not abuse them. Your son may make you so angry that you feel like you could strangle him. But it is not Gods will that you should inflict bodily damage to your son. There is a difference between punishment and discipline. Punishment inflicts pain and discipline instills wisdom. One of the best ways to teach your son something is to discipline him. Don't just yell at him, scold him and put a belt to him. It may make you feel good, but I doubt he will learn anything. But if you discipline him, make him think about what he has done, he will have learned something. Read Hebrews 12:5-13

REFLECTIVE QUESTIONS:

1. IS DOING THE WILL OF GOD YOUR NUMBER ONE PRIORITY IN YOUR LIFE? WHY OR WHY NOT?

2. WHAT ELSE COULD YOU DO TO MAKE JESUS CHRIST YOUR LORD AND SAVIOR?

3. DO YOU WORSHIP THE LORD WITH YOUR SON? DO YOU REGULARLY ATTEND CHURCH? WHY OR WHY NOT?

4. DOES YOUR CHILD KNOW WHO YOU ARE? WHY OR WHY NOT?

5. DO YOU SPEND QUALITY TIME WITH YOUR SON? WHY OR WHY NOT?

6. WHAT ARE THE SACRIFICES THAT YOU MAKE ONBEHALF OF YOUR SON?

7. IF YOU WERE ABRAHAM WHAT WOULD YOU DO?

FATHER JACOB

Jacob name means trickster, hustler, con artist and player. Jacob was a manipulator who tried to do things his own way instead of trusting God. His mother Rebekah helped him steal his Brother Esau's birthright. Jacob had 12 sons who established the 12 tribes of Israel. As a father, he favored his son Joseph, causing jealousy among his brothers. Joseph had a dream of being so powerful that his brothers and parents would bow to him. His father did not like the dream. His jealous brothers despised Joseph and his dream. They threw him in the pit and sold him to the Egyptians.

It appears that Jacob did not treat Joseph right. When Joseph told his father about his dream of personal greatness, his father rejected it. He was not supportive of Joseph and his dream. He could have spoken words of encouragement and assisted Joseph in the fulfillment of his dream. This father did not encourage his son. Jacob dismissed Joseph and his dream which could have emboldened his sons to attack Joseph. Father Jacob did not throw his son into the pit but he did throw away his dream. We fathers can learn for Jacobs's critical mistake.

1. Fathers' must encourage their sons to dream and have great vision for themselves.
2. Fathers' must not play favorites with their children.
3. Fathers must not encourage sibling rivalry and competition.
4. Fathers must develop peace and harmony in the home.
5. The bible says, "Where there is no vision the people perish." The brothers of Joseph perished into the abyss of jealousy and hatred. They needed a vision for themselves. It was Jacobs's responsibility to help all his sons create a vision or a purpose for themselves. It is the father's duty to help all of his children discover their vision and purpose in life.

REFLECTIVE QUESTIONS:

1. WHAT ARE YOUR SONS DREAMS? WHAT DOES HE WANT TO BE IN LIFE?

2. DO YOU ENCOURAGE HIS DREAMS, WHY OR WHY NOT?

3. HAVE YOU TAKEN TIME TO HELP YOUR SON TO READ, RESEARCH AND WRITE DOWN HIS DREAM?

4. HAVE YOU DISCOURAGED OR ENCOURAGED HIS DREAMS? WHY OR WHY NOT?

5. HAVE YOU MADE SURE THERE IS NOT ANY JEALOUSY BETWEEN YOUR CHILDREN?

6. HAVE YOU HELPED YOUR SON TO UNDERSTAND THAT HE WILL HAVE TO WORK HARD, STRUGGLE AND SACRIFICE TO OBTAIN HIS DREAM?

7. HAVE YOU PREPARED YOUR SON TO DEAL WITH FRIENDS, FAMILY AND FOES THAT WILL TRY TO END HIS DREAMS? WHAT COULD YOU TELL HIM?

FATHER DAVID

David was a Shepard of Israel, song writer, singer, giant killer, warrior, King of Israel, husband, adulterer, murderer and father. He was a multi-talented, charismatic, dynamic leader. Yet as a great a public figure David was he had troubled personal life. After David committed adultery with Bathsheba, killed her husband Uriah, he was confronted by the prophet Nathan who told him that his family would always suffer because of his unfaithfulness to God. Consequently, his son Absalom constantly attacked him and tried to kill him. Another of David's son raped his sister Tamar. Absalom ended up killed by one of David's soldiers. There was one family tragedy after another. It was all because David lived a sordid life and was paying the consequences of his sins. There are a number of lessons that we receive from David.

1. Fathers cannot live ungodly lives without it effecting their sons. Fathers must set an example for their sons.
2. Fathers need to understand that God is omniscient and omnipresence. Read Psalm 101
3. Fathers must have moral integrity. They cannot act one way in public and another way in their private life. Their sins will catch up with them.
4. Fathers must be willing to sit down with their sons and let them express their feelings.
5. Fathers must beware of the sibling rivalry and create peace in the home.
6. Father must develop their relationship with Jesus Christ that they may be able to develop their relationship with their son.

REFLECTIVE QUESTIONS:

1. ARE YOU SETTING A POSITIVE MORAL EXAMPLE FOR YOUR SON? WHY OR WHY NOT?

2. DO YOU ALLOW YOUR SON TO EXPRESS HIS THOUGHTS AND FEELINGS?

3. DO YOU USE PROFANITY IN FRONT OF YOUR CHILD? ARE YOU WILLING TO STOP?

4. DO YOU USE DRUGS OR ALCHOHAL? ARE YOU WILLING TO STOP?

5. ARE YOU WILLING TO REPENT OF YOUR SINS AND ACCEPT CHRIST AS YOUR LORD AND SAVIOR?

6. ARE YOUR CHILDREN ANGRY AT YOU AND IF SO, HAVE YOU TALKED TO THEM ABOUT IT?

7. DAVID COMMITTED ADULTERY AND IT ULTIMATELY EFFECTED HIS WHOLE FAMILY. IF YOU ARE HAVING AN AFFAIR OUTSIDE OF YOUR MARRIAGE, HOW WILL IT EFFECT YOU, YOUR WIFE AND CHILDREN?

FATHER JOSEPH

Joseph was the husband of Mary and the foster father of Jesus the son of God. Joseph was a righteous, humble man of God who protected and provided for Jesus Christ. There is not much said or written about Joseph. The biblical writers emphasized Jesus' Heavenly Father and not Joseph. But that should not diminish the enormous contribution that Joseph made in raising Jesus. Joseph was responsible for raising, nurturing, teaching, counseling and guiding Jesus. He did not get a lot of recognition for it. But he still was a wonderful surrogate father for him. Father Joseph teaches todays father how to be a humble, loving and caring father.

1. To be a good father you must be humble, obedient servant.
2. Fathers must be willing to give and sacrifice without praise or recognition.
3. Fathers must understand that their sons have the potential for greatness and they must raise them that way.
4. Joseph had several dreams about his foster son Jesus. You must have a dream or vision for your son.
5. Joseph was willing to uproot himself, leave his home to protect baby Jesus and wife Mary. As a father you have a responsibility to do whatever is necessary to protect your family.
6. In difficult times, Joseph was righteous and obedient to God. As a father you must have a solid relationship with God. Like Joseph, you must obey God even when you don't understand His will.

REFLECTIVE QUESTIONS:

1. DO YOU HAVE A RELATIONSHIP WITH JESUS CHRIST?

2. ARE YOU WILLING TO BE A HUMBLE, OBEDIENT PARENT WHO RARELY IS PRAISED OR ACKNOWLEDGED?

3. WHAT ARE YOU DOING TO ENSURE YOUR SONS SAFTEY? ARE YOU WILLING TO MOVE OUT OF THE NEIGHBORHOOD? WHY OR WHY NOT?

4. WRITE ABOUT THE GREATNESS THAT YOU SEE IN YOUR SON?

5. WHAT IS YOUR DREAM OR VISION ABOUT YOUR SON?

6. WHAT IS YOUR SONS DREAM OR VISION ABOUT HIMSELF?

MOTHER REBEKAH

Rebekah was the wife of Isaac. For a long time she could not have any children. In Israel to be without children was a badge of shame. A motherless child was disrespected and disdained. It was thought that a motherless child was cursed by God. Fortunately her husband Isaac prayed for her and God blessed them with the birth of twin sons Esau and Jacob. Rebekah rejoiced over her miraculous birth and she thanked God for her sons. Unfortunately, she favored one son over another. She plotted and planned with her son Jacob to steal Esau's' birthright. Consequently there was a family feud between the brothers. Esau and Jacob became enemies and did not reconcile until they were old men. What are the lessons we learn from this mother?

1. Mothers should never play favorites with their children. It causes too much sibling rivalry.
2. Mothers should help each child understand that they are special. Every child has their own birth right, talents, personality and abilities. It's up to the mother to help every child discover their God given potential.
3. Rebekah plotted and planned to deceive her son Esau and her husband Isaac. Her deviousness eventually back fired. Mothers must have an open conversations with their son and spouse. Discuss issues and concerns openly. Ask your son how he is feeling. Tell your husband what is going on with his son.
4. Rebekah did not talk to her husband about her plan to steal Esau's birth right. Mothers must take the initiative to talk to their son's father if there are problems. A lack of communication between parents only makes matters worse.

REFLECTIVE QUESTIONS:

1. WHO IS YOUR FAVOURITE CHILD AND WHY?

2. IS THERE SIBLING RIVALRY IN YOUR FAMILY AND WHAT ARE YOU DOING ABOUT IT?

3. WHAT ARE YOU DOING TO CREATE PEACE AND HARMONY IN THE HOME?

4. HOW CAN YOU GET YOUR FAMILY TO COMMUNICATE BETTER WITH EACH OTHER?

5. WHO IS YOUR SON ANGRY WITH AND WHY?

6. HOW CAN YOU TEACH YOUR SON TO BE HONEST WITH HIMSELF, YOU AND OTHERS?

7. HAVE YOU HELPED YOUR SON TO UNDERSTAND JEALOUSY AND HOW TO COPE WITH IT?

MOTHER JOCHEBED

Jochebed is the mother of Moses. She is an unsung heroine of the faith. It took enormous faith in God to set her baby adrift on the Nile River. Jochebed wanted to preserve her son Moses from the mass slaughter of Hebrew boys. So she made a basket, placed baby Moses in it and gently placed it in the river, hoping someone would find him and raise him. Pharaohs daughter found Moses, adopted him and had his mother be his nurse. Later God used Moses to liberate the Hebrews from Egyptian bondage and take them to the Promise land. But none of it would be possible if it was not for the tremendous faith of Mother Jochebed. What lessons do we learn from her?

1. Mother Jochebed had faith to see greatness in her baby. Mothers must have faith to see greatness in their sons.
2. Mother Jochebed had faith to protect her baby from the Pharaohs army. Mothers must have faith to protect their sons from the evils of the world.
3. Mother Jochebed had faith to put baby Moses in a basket and into Nile River. Mothers must have faith to let go and let God protect their sons.
4. Mother Jochebed had faith to stay in the life of baby Moses. Mothers must have faith to find ways to participate in the life of their sons.
5. Read the following scriptures Hebrews 11

REFLECTIVE QUESTIONS

1. DO YOU HAVE THE FAITH TO SEE THE GREATNESS IN YOUR SON?

2. DO YOU HAVE THE FAITH TO PROTECT YOUR SON? WHAT ARE YOU DOING TO PROTECT HIM?

3. DO YOU HAVE THE FAITH TO LET GO AND LET GOD? HOW ARE YOU DEMONSTRATING YOUR TRUST IN GOD?

4. HOW ARE YOU HELPING YOUR SON TO BE A GREAT PERSON ONE DAY?

5. YOUR SON COULD BE A GREAT LEADER ONEDAY. HOW ARE YOU DEVELOPING HIM FOR IT?

MOTHER MARY

Mary the mother of Jesus is the most honored woman of the bible. She is the human mother of Jesus, the Savior of the world. She was humble young woman who accepted the will of God in her life. She was a virgin who was impregnated by the Holy Spirit. Some people doubted her story. Even her husband Joseph doubted. Some must have thought she was either insane, a dreamer or psychologically imbalanced. But Mary kept the faith and gave birth to the son of God and never doubted him. Her son was criticized, vilified, persecuted and crucified. Mary never left his side. She was there for him to the bitter end. Mother Mary can teach today's mother about love and long suffering.

1. Mother must love their sons unconditionally. They maybe thugs, drug addicts, car jackers and ex-convicts or criminals. No matter who they are and what they have done a mothers love is there.
2. Mothers must be long suffering. They must exhibit patience and understanding.
3. Mothers must have faith to believe that God can do the impossible.
4. Mothers must never lose hope that God can resurrect their son.

REFLECTIVE QUESTIONS:

1. HOW HAVE YOU SHOWED UNCONDITIONAL LOVE TO YOUR SON?

2. IN WHAT WAYS ARE YOU LONG SUFFERING TOWARD YOUR SON?

3. WHY DO YOU BELIEVE THAT GOD CAN DO THE IMPOSSIBLE WITH YOUR SON?

4. DO YOU HAVE THE FAITH TO STAND WITH YOUR SON THROUGH HIS CRUCIFIXION?

5. DO YOU HAVE THE HOPE TO BELIEVE THAT YOUR SON WILL BE RESURRECTED FROM SPIRITUAL DEATH IE. DRUGS, ALCHOHAL, CRIMINAL BEHAVIOR, UNEMPLOYMENT, POOR GRADES, GANG ACTIVITY OR SEXUAL PROMISCUITY? WHY?

PIETY FOR PARENTS

It takes a lot of spiritual strength to be a parent. Parenting an unsaved, undisciplined young African American male can be demanding on your heart, mind and soul. The world is designed to bring him down while you are trying to raise him up. This tug and war battle between the worlds ways and Gods' way can take its toll on you. Even the strongest saints of God get tired some time. During those trying times it is good to meditate on the Word of God. Every parent needs to develop a sense of piety to become better parents. You need to take time out of your busy schedule and develop a devotional lifestyle that will replenish your weary soul. The Bible is a source of spiritual strength and wisdom for every parent. There is a word of encouragement for every parent and every situation. The following scriptures are categorized for a parent's particular spiritual need. Read, reflect and pray that God will use His Word to strengthen, heal and guide you.

PARENTING AND PATIENCE

"And let us not grow weary in well doing for in due season you shall reap if you faint not." Galatians 6:9

"Let us hold fast the confession of our hope without wavering for He is who promised is faithful." Hebrews 10:23

"My brethren count it all joy when you fall into various trials knowing that the testing of your faith produces patience. But let patience have its perfect work that you may be perfect and complete lacking nothing." James 1:2-4

"Therefore be patient brethren until the coming of the Lord. See how the farmer waits for the precious fruit of the earth until it receives the early and latter rain. You also be patient. Establish your hearts for the coming of the Lord is at hand." James 5:7, 8

PARENTING ANGER AND FRUSTRATION

"Fathers, do not provoke your children to anger, but bring them up in the discipline and instruction of the Lord." Ephesians 6:4

"My Christian brothers, you know that everyone should listen much and speak little. He should be slow to become angry. A man's' anger does not allow him to be right with God." James 1:19-20

"Do not be quick in spirit to be angry. For anger is in the heart of fools." Ecclesiastes 7:9

"He who has a quick temper acts in a foolish way, and a man who makes sinful plans is hated." Proverbs 14:17

"A man of anger starts fights, and a man with a bad temper is full of wrong doing." Proverbs 29:22

"Stop being angry. Turn away from fighting. Do not trouble yourself. It leads to wrong doing." Psalm 37:8

"A gentle answer turns away anger, but a sharp word causes anger." Proverbs 15:1

"If you are angry, do not let it become sin. Get over your anger before the day is finished." Ephesians 4:26

PARENTING AND FAITH

"Now faith is the substance of things hoped for and the evidence of things not seen." Hebrews 11:1

"But without faith it is impossible to please Him, for he who comes to God must believe that He is a rewarder of those who diligently seek Him." Hebrews 11:6

"For we walk by faith not by sight." II. Corinthians 5:7

"Faith comes by hearing and hearing by the Word of God."

PARENTING AND GODS' GUIDANCE

"Seek first His Kingdom and His Righteousness and all those things shall be added unto you."Matthew 6:33

"Trust in the Lord with all thine heart and lean not to thine own understanding and He shall give thee the desires of thine heart." Proverbs 3:5-7

"I will instruct you and teach you in the way you should go. I will guide you with my eye." Psalm 32:8

"With Him are wisdom and strength, He has counsel and understanding." Job 12:13

"If any of you lack wisdom, let him ask of God, who gives to all liberally and without reproach, and it will be given to him." James 1:5

PARENTING AND PRAYER

"And all things, whatever you ask in prayer, believing you will receive." Matthew 21:22

"If you abide in me, and my words abide in you, you will ask what you desire, and it shall be done for you." John 15:7

"And whatever you ask in my name, that I will do, that the Father may be glorified in the Son. If you ask anything in my name, I will do it." John 14:13-14

"And the prayer of faith will save the sick, and the Lord will raise him up. And if he has committed sins, he will be forgiven. Confess your trespasses to one another, and pray for one another, that you may be healed. The effective fervent prayer of a righteous man avails much." James 5:15-16

"Now this is the confidence that we have in him, that if we ask anything according to His will, He hears us. And if we know He hears us, whatever we ask, we know that we have petitions that we have asked of Him." I .John 5:14, 15

"He will call upon me, and I will answer him, I will be with him in time of trouble; I will deliver him and honor him." Psalm 91:15

"Ask, and it will be given you; seek, and you will find: knock, and it will be opened to you. For everyone who asks receives, and he who seeks finds, and to him who knocks it will be opened. If you then being evil, know how to give good gifts to your children, how much more will your father who is in heaven give good things to those who ask Him." Matthew 7:7-8, 11

PARENTING AND DISCIPLINE

"Do not withhold discipline from a child, if you strike him with a rod, he will not die. If you strike him with the rod, you will save his soul from Sheol." Proverbs 22:13, 14

"Train up a child in the way he should go, even when he is old he will not depart from it." Proverbs 22:6

"Discipline your son, and he will give you rest, he will give delight to your heart." Proverbs 29:17

"The rod and reproof give wisdom, but a child left to himself brings shame to his mother." Proverbs 29:15

"Whoever spares the rod hates his son, but he who loves him is diligent to discipline him." Proverbs 13:24

"It is for discipline that you have to endure. God is treating you as sons. For what son is there whom his father does not discipline?" Hebrews 12:7

"Folly is bound up in the heart of a child, but the rod of discipline drives it far from him." Proverbs 22:15

"For the Lord reproves him whom he loves, as a father the son in whom he delights." Proverbs 3:12

"Discipline your son, for there is hope, do not set your heart on putting him to death." Proverbs 19:18

PARENTING AND TEACHING

"Hear, O Israel. The Lord our God, the Lord is one. You shall love the Lord your God with all your heart and with all your soul and all your might. And these words that I command you today shall be upon your heart. You shall teach them diligently to your children, and shall talk of them when you sit in your house, and when you walk by the way, and when you lie down and when you rise. You shall bind them as a sign on your head and they shall be frontlets between your eyes. You shall write them on the doorposts of your house and on your gates." Deuteronomy 6: 4-9

"Hear, my son, your father's instruction and forsake not your mothers teaching. For they are a grace garland for your head and pendants for your neck." Proverbs 1:8-9

"My son, keep my words and treasure my commandments with you. Keep my commandments and live. Keep my teaching as the apple of your eye, bind them on your fingers, and write them on the tablet of your heart." Proverbs 7:1-3

"Older women likewise are to be reverent in behavior not slanderers or slaves to much wine. They are to teach what is good." Titus 2:3

"You shall teach them to your children, talking of them when you are sitting in your house, and when you are walking by the way and when you lie down, and when you rise" Deuteronomy 11:19

"Hear this, you elders, give ear, all inhabitants of the land. Has such a thing happened in your days, days of your fathers? Tell your children of it and let your children tell their children and their children to another generation." Joel 1:2-3

"I will open my mouth in a parable. I will utter dark sayings from of old things that we have heard and known, that our fathers have told us. We will not hide them from their children but tell the coming generation the glorious deeds of the Lord and his might and the wonders he has done. He established a testimony in Jacob and appointed a law in Israel, which he commanded our fathers to teach to their children that the next generation might know them, the children yet unborn, and arise and tell them to their children so that they should not be like their fathers a stubborn and rebellious generation, a generation whose heart was not steadfast, whose spirit was not faithful to God." Psalm 78:2-8

"Let no corrupting talk come out of your mouths, but only such as is good for building up, as fits the occasion, that it may give grace to those who hear." Ephesians 4:29

"The living, the living, he thanks you, as I do this day, the father makes known to the children your faithfulness." Isaiah 38:19

"And when in time to come your son will ask you, 'What does this mean?' you shall say to him, By the strong hand of the Lord He brought us out of Egypt, from the house of slavery." Exodus 13:14

"He established a testimony in Jacob and appointed a law in Israel, which he commanded our fathers to teach to their children." Psalm 78:5

"But have stubbornly followed their own hearts and have gone after the Baals, as their fathers taught them." Jeremiah 9:14

A PARENTS TESTIMONY

It is truly an honor and a privilege to be a parent. I am blessed to have an intelligent, independent , pretty , precocious , vivacious , spiritually minded and God fearing daughter named Alexandria Monet White. Also I am blessed to be the father of a bright, insightful , athletic , caring , handsome , comedic , sensitive , kind hearted , soft spoken , mature young gentleman named Samuel White IV. Both of my children are the crown of my life. There aren't enough superlatives that can express my parental pride and joy. They make me laugh. They have taught me how to love. They have helped me to be a parent. They are wonderful children. But I could not be the parent that I am and the children could not be the children that they are if it were not for their mother. My wife and their mother is a "virtuous woman" who not only "brings home the bacon, but she cooks it as well." She raised, nutured, taught and discipline the children and worked a full time job. If it wasn't for her industrious, indomitable spirit the children would not be as intelligent, insightful, and godly. She has done an outstanding job raising our children and the credit belongs to her. I give God and my wife all praise and glory.

Bibliography

Bach, Julia S.   Drug Abuse: St. Paul, MN:
Opposing Viewpoints.   Greenhaven Press, 1988.

Beattie, Melody.   Co-dependent No   New York: Harper &
More.   Row, 1987.

Benson, Janice.   Black Children.   Baltimore: John Hopkins
Press, 1982.

Beschner, George,   Teen Drug Use.   Lexington, MA:
and Friedman,   Lexington Books, 1986.
Alfred.

Clark, Kenneth.   Prejudice and Your   Middletown, CT:
Child.   Wesleyan University
Press.

Cohen, Albert.   Delinquent Boys. The   Glencoe, IL: The Free
Culture of the Gang.   Press, 1955.

Comer, James.   "Educating Poor   Scientific American, 259
Minority Children."   (November, 1988).

Cone, James H.   God of the Oppressed.   New York: Seabury Press,
1973.

Cottle, Thomas.   Black Children,   Boston: Houghton
White Dreams.   Mifflin, 1974.

Cully, Iris F.   Christian Child   San Francisco: Harper &
Development.   Row, 1979.

Diner, Claudia.	Chemical Dependency.	St. Paul, MN: Green Haven Press, 1985.
DuPont, Robert.	Getting Tough on Gateway Drugs: A Guide for Family.	Washington D.C.: American Psychiatric Press, 1984.
Finley, Dean.	Handbook for Youth Evangelism.	Nashville: Broadman Press, 1988.
Glasgow, Douglas.	The Black Underclass.	New York: Vintage Books, 1980.
Gold, Martin.	Delinquent Behavior in an American City.	Belmont, CA: Brooks/Cole, 1970.
Grier, William, and Cobbs, Price.	Black Rage.	New York: Basic Books, 1968.
Hare, Nathan.	Bringing the Black Boy to Manhood: The Passage.	San Francisco: The Black Think Tank, 1985.
Jones, Kenneth.	Black Adolescents.	Berkeley, CA: Cobb & Henry, 1989.
June, Lee.	The Black Family.	Grand Rapids, MI: Zondervan Publishing, 1991.
Klein, Malcolm.	Street Gangs and Street Workers.	Englewood Cliffs, NJ: Prentice Hall, 1971.
Kunjufu, Jawanza.	Countering the Conspiracy to Destroy Black Boys.	Chicago, IL: African American Images, 1985.
_____.	Countering the Conspiracy to Destroy Black Boys Vol. II.	Chicago, IL: African American Images, 1984.

_____. Developing Positive Self-Images and Discipline in Black Children. Chicago, IL: African American Images, 1984.

_____. Motivating and Preparing Black Youth to Work. Chicago, IL: African American Images, 1986.

_____. To Be Popular or Smart. Chicago, IL: African American Images.

Schwendinger, Julia. Adolescent Subcultures and Delinquency. New York: Praeger, 1985.

Shockley, Grant. Working with Black Youth. Nashville: Abingdon Press, 1989.

Stewart, Carlyle. God, Being and Liberation. New York: University Press of America, 1989.

Taylor, Carl. Dangerous Society. East Lansing, MI: Michigan State University Press, 1990.

Wilson, William. The Truly Disadvantaged. Chicago, IL: University of Chicago Press, 1987.

White, Van Henri. Frustration in America. Rochester New York,

Perkins, James. 12 Plays for Boys. Judson Press

About the Author

Dr. Samuel White, III is a native of Rochester New York and the son of the late Samuel White II and Anna White. Dr. White graduated with honors from Brockport State College with a Bachelor of Science degree. He went on to graduate from Harvard Divinity School with a Masters of Theological Studies degree and a Masters of Divinity degree from the Methodist Theological School in Ohio. He completed his educational pursuits by achieving a Doctorate of Ministry degree from Drew University. He has been an adjunct professor at the Ecumenical Theological School, Mary Grove College and William Tyndale College. Dr. White has been the recipient of numerous civic and religious awards. He was awarded Minister of the Year Award, The Rev. Charles Hill Award from the Michigan Progressive Baptist Convention and The Presidents' Award from the Progressive Baptist Convention. Dr. White served as the President of the Michigan Progressive Baptist Convention. He is currently the senior Pastor of the Friendship Baptist Church and a Hospice Chaplain for Henry Ford. He is a preacher, teacher, revivalist, motivational speaker, pastoral care counselor, leadership trainer, grief group facilitator and writer. He published, "It is Well with My Soul, Spiritual Care for the Dying" and it can be purchased online at Westbow Press, Barnes & Noble and Amazon. com. Dr. White is happily married to the former Sandra Wilson and they are blessed with two children Alexandria and Samuel IV.